$0 to $1,000,000 in 365 Days!

An Entrepreneur's True Story

Robert G. Wajda

Formatting Editor: Jonathan Gullery E-Mail: jg@midcity.net
Cover Design: Michael Cox E-Mail: Michael@michaelcox.com

ISBN 0-615-12041-5

Wajda Publishing
Jacksonville, FL 32207

On the World Wide Web at http://www.0to1million.com/

To my divine wife and companion Mayra

.

Table of Contents

Chapter 4 - *Your Keys to Success*

Chapter 5 - *Ways to Save Money Using the Internet*

Chapter 6 - *Internet Placement, Registration, and Marketing*

Chapter 7 - Final Review

How this Book Can Benefit You

My journey began several years ago when I made a risky business move. I wanted a career change, so I jumped in and entered an unknown market. Soon I discovered I had a special talent for making every company I touched an instant success.

For several years, I observed my new clients' sales figures that came from the work I did for them. I noticed these clients were earning hundreds of thousands of dollars from the couple of thousand-dollar investments they had made in me.

I soon realized it was possible to generate more than one million dollars in sales in just one year with the right clients. To do that, I had to dedicate the necessary time and make the commitment to make it happen, but one step at a time. I also decided that I wasn't about to participate in such achievement unless I was included in the profits.

I was so confident of what I could accomplish that I decided to risk everything by investing most of my time in the one company that had been the most honest and faithful to me and only keep a handful of other clients. I wanted to generate one million dollars in sales in 365 days with these few clients, and that is exactly what I did!

This true and remarkable story shows that fulfilling a business dream is possible. I outline the easy, self-proving steps anyone can take to make the most out of a business venture. My book is a learning map that can make any business a great success.

By studying every aspect of what I did and applying it to your own individual business situation, you can discover that successful "unique" market that has no competition. You can learn my simple but workable techniques, such as, "How to Change One Letter in Your Business Name to Earn an Extra one hundred thousand dollars in Sales on the Internet."

I have made the story of my business journey part autobiography and part "How -to Guide," which will keep you excited and involved throughout the book.

Chapter 1

The Beginning of the Journey

The Journey

My journey from $0 to $1,000,000 began back in 1994 when I realized I was just not happy working for the company I had been employed by for the last 7 years. I had climbed the corporate ladder about as far as I could and was suddenly faced with a question many of you may be faced with right now, "What do I do next?" Was I to stay where I was and settle for the lifestyle I had created, or strike out and try something else? The question, "What do I do next?" is the first test everyone must take to actually determine for yourself whether you've really got what it takes to become a self-employed entrepreneur. Believe it or not, about five percent of the population discovers they can answer that question. The other ninety-five percent ends up working for the five percent that can.

I always knew I had what it takes to go into business for myself. I then realized I was just waiting for the right time. I had a little money saved up, and the only thing I knew for sure was that I would not be happy working for anybody else ever again. One bitterly cold September night, at about three o'clock in the morning, I was taking a break in the snowy parking lot outside the large photo-processing factory where I worked. For several weeks, I had tried to convince myself that I really needed to move on and start a new career for myself. As the defroster from my car started melting the ice from the windshield, I saw the stars shining as brightly as I had ever seen them. An overwhelming feeling came across me and I said, "Tonight is the night I'm going to walk out and start all over."

At that instant, I made a promise to myself—Never work for anyone else for the rest of my life. When my 15-minute break was over, I walked into my workplace and smiled at everyone as I walked to my station. I slowly gathered all my belongings from my locker and went straight to the supervisor's office. Keep in mind that I had hundreds of friends at this company, and this workplace was the only lifestyle I had ever known.

As I handed in my belongings, I clearly remember saying, "It is time for me to move on. I am starting my own business—I quit!" The two main supervisors didn't know what to say. I was such a good employee, and the job—for the area—was such a good one, no one could believe what I had just said. In the small town I lived in and with the economy struggling, anyone that did what I just did would have been assumed to be a little crazy.

Little did I know that the decision I made at three o'clock that morning would forever change not only my life, but the lives of many other people as well. It did not occur to me at the time that I would have the chance to help so many people.

The Previous Year

About a year before that fateful night, I had filed for a Patent on a high-tech security device at the United States Patent and Trademark Office. The Patent had just been issued right before I quit, and I decided to make this device into my first business. I knew the only way to make the business a success was to do one of two things: either sell my Patent rights or manufacture the product myself. Since it would cost about two hundred thousand dollars to manufacture the product, and I just didn't have the extra two hundred thousand lying around, I decided instead to try to license the product to a manufacturer.

I searched the Thomas Register for all manufacturers that I thought fit into the category, and I contacted corporations all around the world. Surprisingly, the response I received from almost all of them was remarkably similar, "We love your product, Mr. Wajda, and we believe it will be a success, but we just don't have current resources to fund it." This scenario kept repeating itself until my fifteen thousand dollar savings account was almost at zero. At that time, I said to myself, "I better put this one on the back burner and figure out something else before I go completely broke. I don't think that is too far away!"

Starting a Business with Research

It was on that very day my second business was born, an Internet Reselling Company. In the summer of 1996, I decided that I was going to build web sites for businesses and try to find a way to earn a living with a monthly residual from them. The only problem was that I didn't know anything about web sites or even how to build them! This was the time period when entirely new ISP's (Internet Service Providers) were popping up everywhere. I believed that, if I only had the resources and funding to get started, I would be right up there with all the rest of those bright new entrepreneurs.

For two weeks, I researched everything I could about business, web sites, e-commerce, and how the Internet worked. I found a way to resell server space and make a monthly profit. I learned how to build web sites as well as how to buy a web site authoring program.

Basically, I started by making some business cards and passing them out all over town. I remember leaving them at service stations, community bulletin boards, and everywhere I could get away with leaving them. Next, I printed out about two hundred flyers about my services and got two hundred names from the business yellow pages and sent them out. It didn't take very long for the telephone to start ringing.

After I secured a new client, I would purchase server space from a large web hosting company for a few dollars a month for each domain name I had. Then I could resell the domain names for one hundred dollars a month for each account. "What a wonderful business idea," I thought to myself. Purchase web space for a few dollars a month for an account, build a web site for a client, and make a profit there; best of all, after the web site was built, I could then charge the client one hundred dollars a month for web site hosting and maintenance. I was making ninety dollars month profit from each client!

I generated a whopping two hundred dollars in my first month in business! I was so happy. I had generated this money all on my own. It's interesting that, today, everyone wants to get rich without having to really work for the money. Now I think back to those early days. The basic fundamentals that made my company a success are the same fundamentals that make not only my company successful today, but also my clients' businesses successful as well.

If you haven't already guessed it, those "two weeks of research" I did prior to starting my company coupled with my determination actually were a big part of its success then and my continuing success to this day. By carefully researching every possible avenue and direction I could take, I discovered that research was what made my company a success. To this day, I spend just as much time researching the information about what I am about to do as I spend doing work it takes to complete the job.

The Internet Boom

The Internet boom "boomed," but then what happened? I'll tell you what happened. A lot of deep pocket investors and companies jumped into an unknown market without doing virtually any research. Can you imagine the company you now work for spending two million dollars on a project that had no track record and hired fifty additional employees at a hefty six-digit monthly payroll increase?

Further, all the work these employees did for this new project generated absolutely nothing in returns. What a waste of money! I often wish I could have managed just a few of those companies that had that much cash to throw away. People actually thought then—and many still do—that spending a lot of money on a high-tech Internet Web Site complete with the latest in bells and whistles will somehow automatically result in a successful, profitable site. This "vision of success" is so far from the truth it is not even funny!

It's amazing. The only thing most people hear about the Internet is that a lot of the large companies did not make it. In my case, I have seen more successes than you can imagine.

In order to have a profitable web presence, the very first thing a company must do is to treat the web site as a business, have faith in your ideas, and never give up. A web site can actually generate more money than your existing business—if it is put together and managed effectively.

Planning Your Business

Most people would not start a regular business without a Business and Marketing Plan. Would you? Well, the rules are the same for a web site; only these businesses have higher rewards with lower overhead. Any web presence without a sound Business and/or Marketing Plan is doomed to fail even before it starts up. (Of course, a few—maybe one percent—get lucky, but are you willing to take that chance? The odds are lousy!)

Most people do not consider this first critical step as something that is important. People want results and want them fast. These people need to learn that the important step of paying someone to help them create a Marketing/Business Plan and spending a little money up front to do it just so, could actually generate for them a little thirty thousand a year bonus. You can't get "there" if you don't know where you are going, if you don't know where "there" is. Research is so important that it's a mystery why most companies are not willing to spend the extra dollars and time up front to buy the needed extra time to figure out exactly what they want to accomplish. If the purpose is not defined, the result doesn't matter.

Every time I have accepted a new client, I have spent days analyzing what needed to be done, how that was going to be done, what the competition was, how much it would cost, how much traffic to expect, what placement would be received, and how soon the ROI (Return on Investment or how much time it will take to get your investment back) would be met. These are basic fundamental issues or truths that should be studied before you start any business venture. This initial research is crucial, and throughout this book, I will explain to you—step by step—how this task can be accomplished to be most effective.

How Much Money Should You Spend?

There is no easy formula to figure out how much money you should spend and where you should spend it, but I will give you some examples that will guide you in the right direction. Let's say, for example, a small new startup company wants to start a new e-commerce business and web site, and they have about ten thousand dollars to spend on this new project. Most companies would spend about nine thousand on the web site itself and try to register, promote, and market it for the remaining one thousand. Sounds like a good plan, doesn't it? Not at all! If the same company spent one thousand on the web site and the remaining nine thousand dollars in promoting it with the right company, techniques, and staff, that same site would be ten times more successful! The same investment spent more effectively makes all the difference.

The concept sounds very simple, but about ninety-five percent of all new web presences make the same mistake over and over. People just seem to think they must have the flashiest web site on the Internet. And yet, many people—and I include myself in that number—find several of these flashy web sites to be very annoying! Consider the success of the Pet Rock as a good case in point. Since Pet Rocks cost hardly anything to devise, the company was able to spend millions promoting its concept. I'm sure you know what I am talking about. The miniature pets that you water and grow hair are another marketing success story. These are just not the type of products that people would normally run to their local stores to purchase. In each case, it was the marketing strategy that resulted in success.

Understanding Market Trends

After being in business for about four years, I considered myself a pretty successful businessman. I was consistently averaging over one hundred thousand dollars a year, even though I usually spent most of it. I was still pretty much a happy camper. As the Internet became more and more competitive, I knew that I must either make a career change or start doing something very different to continue my success. I have always seemed to know when market trends were about to change, and I have always been one step ahead of my competition.

I started looking at exactly where I was and what changes I could make to continue my success and to take it a little farther. It was then that I noticed something very similar about most of my clients. The little bit of work that I was doing for them was making them all very profitable.

One client, in particular, was making about one hundred thousand dollars plus in her retail store. Not bad for a small business. I built and designed a web site for this client for about three thousand dollars and charged her about one hundred dollars per month as a server and consultant fee. The consultant fee was my "retainer" for keeping an eye on the web site and the clients informed on new trends in the market. I was to guide them in the right direction. Does one hundred dollars a month sound like a lot of money for what I did for her? With the successful implementation of the new web site along with my marketing strategies and techniques, this client brought in an extra two hundred and fifty thousand dollars in revenue—from that one three thousand dollar web site I built!

What a deal! I give this company a three thousand dollar web site, and it makes the company an extra quarter of a million dollars a year in sales. The company made all that extra money—not me. To me, there was something very wrong with that picture.

By paying attention, I then noticed another pattern among the clients I had made so incredibly profitable. After being with me for about a year, they would start complaining that their monthly server fees were too high. After all, they could have their sites hosted for twenty dollars a month at "Bargain Corner dot com" or some such cheap hosting service. "What a slap in the face!" I thought.

Almost every one of these clients ended up getting very greedy and thinking they no longer needed my services. They would then transfer their profitable web sites to another server to save money! They forgot all about what had brought them there in the first place—my good ideas and me! It is so amazing. Once a company becomes used to success —not to mention all that extra cash—they seem to start believing that they actually accomplished it all on their own. They seem to think that they themselves are the brilliant ones who made it all happen.

This scenario has happened to me more than a dozen times over the years. It was getting to the point where, six months before a client would make a move to transfer their site, I would already know what they were about to do. I would know this by some of the questions they would start asking me. They became so excited that they started asking me questions like, "how do you do this?" and "what server do you use?" — questions they really shouldn't have been asking me about my business. After all, I never asked them where they bought their products so cheap or how they managed to do what they do. Basically, it was really none of my business. They all found what I did for them so exciting that they just could not resist the temptation of trying knock to me out of the picture and do it all themselves.

I would find similar clients in the same field and make their competitors' web sites more profitable than the ones I had built for them. These former clients forgot one very important thing. It was my techniques that had put them at the top and guided them in the correct direction. My unique techniques gave them the business that made them rich. I thought, "If I can do this for them, wouldn't they be smart enough to realize I could do it for their competitors as well?" Unfortunately for some, they weren't smart enough!

I was so good at this game that, every now and then and just for the fun of it, I would accept new clients and make them rich already knowing what they would do many months down the road. I'd give the client a better e-commerce business than the one that had just canceled my services, sending the one that canceled me to the poorhouse or at least back to where they had started. After completing this process a few times, I decided I have had enough. Yes, it was fun at the time, but I just wasn't getting anywhere myself.

I decided to take all my knowledge and experience and

offer it as a continuing consulting service for those that could comply with my terms. That's right. If I honestly knew that I could triple a company's sales via e-commerce, then I could actually write my own paycheck and have a lot more control of everything that was really going on.

A New Vision

Even though I have personally published tens of thousands of web pages and directories on the Internet, any bright kid could build a better web site than I can. Making a web site generate some serious cash is where my expertise comes into play. Now I found myself visiting potential new clients with a vision and a plan to get them making a specific return on their investment! It was going to cost them a lot more up front, and they would have to commit to a large, pre-signed monthly consulting fee and royalties as well. This was the perfect solution to the business problems I was having with clients leaving after they got a little greedy.

I would visit a potential new client and offer them the opportunity to make their business more successful. Since I have learned so much on the Internet over the years, I could truthfully say I have a great track record with my clients. I pretty much know which ones can be successful and which ones will fail before I even start. I decided I would not even take on a client if I did not think I could help them. To summarize where I was and where I was going is quite simple. I used to be at the mercy of the client. Now I have restructured my business so that the client and I are locked together. Their success is my success!

A typical proposal would go something like this. Instead of me delivering this long proposal on what I could do for my potential clients and telling them how much it was going to cost them, I placed myself in control of the business proposals. I would set up an initial meeting with a potential client that was referred to me. I would travel to see them and have an hour or so meeting discovering exactly what they do and what they are currently selling on the Internet. Since I know that ninety nine percent of all web sites cannot even pay for themselves, I found myself at an incredible advantage.

I would take some notes from our initial meeting and look them over to determine if I could actually make their web site profitable. Over the years, I have developed a special formula that allows me to determine if a client can be successful on the Internet or not.

At this point, I would do one of two things. I would either give the client a call and let them know that there was nothing I could do for them, OR I would give them a call and tell them I would create a free marketing plan for them that would take me about two weeks to complete. The marketing plan I would submit would be pretty basic. It would not divulge any strategies, secrets, or even an idea of how I was going to do what I said I was going to do. One thing you should always remember in business—you should not, under any circumstances, give away all of your secrets. Save the absolute best ones for yourself.

Basically, I would outline my strategy in a ten-page preliminary marketing plan. This plan would be comprised of market share, current competition, preliminary marketing, and other information that will be explained in more detail in another chapter. By the time I completely researched their company, I would know not only the market share, but also the profit margins and exactly how much profit could be made from each sale.

At the end of my marketing proposal, I would have released in detail the sales expectations for the next year. I would no longer tell the client how much I would charge them for doing all of this work. Instead, I would tell them what I could make for their company in additional gross sales by utilizing my services. In order for me to actually progress this far in a proposal, I would have to have one hundred percent confidence in what I was proposing.

In addition, a typical proposal would state what expectations in dollars the client could expect to receive by taking me on as a consultant. Furthermore, the proposal would also state that I would not charge them one penny in fees for my services. Instead, I would work on a commission basis in the form of a percentage.

Now, a lot of you are probably thinking, "How in the world can someone do this and actually make a profit?" The plan is actually more unique and creative than you may think. Let's say, for example, I proposed that I could generate for a certain company an additional ten thousand dollars in sales, and the company agreed to pay me fifteen percent off the top of every penny that was brought in as a result of their utilizing my services. Well, the typical company has been on the Internet for several years, and they are not selling much of anything every month. If they used my services, at least they would be making something.

Imagine a consultant coming to this company and saying, "I want to make you an additional ten thousand dollars a month in sales, and I will do all the internet marketing and work, and I will only charge you fifteen percent of what is sold off your web site." It doesn't take a rocket scientist to figure out that this company would pay me one thousand five hundred dollars a month if I could generate the numbers I said I could. The numbers would not bother them either because they had never made it before. Now let's say I took it a little further and generated one hundred thousand dollars a month in sales instead of only ten thousand! My commissions would then reach fifteen thousand per month. That's not too bad for a consultant, is it?

These are the type of business deals that I have been engaged in over the past years, and I had several months in which my commissions were over fifteen thousand dollars! It is a win/win situation for both parties involved. Let's face it. There are not many consultants that can generate an extra one hundred thousand dollars in sales per month for companies, and there are not many businesses that would turn down an additional eighty five thousand dollars in revenue a month for letting some optimistic guy run their web site.

Chapter 2

Getting Starting by Understanding E-Commerce

Getting Started

The first thing you must accomplish in operating a successful e-commerce web presence is to understand what e-commerce is. In my experience, I have discovered that successful e-commerce web sites have two things in common. First, in order to have a successful e-commerce company, you have to have a quality product or service. In addition, you should have something you can offer your customers that is completely different and unique that your competition offers. Such a product completes one of the requirements for a successful web presence. Without a good quality product or service, your business is doomed to fail before it even starts.

Secondly, your company must be able to generate quality web traffic in terms of people visiting your site. You must be able to get their attention, so they will return to your web site and tell their friends. This step may sound like a very simple one to accomplish; however, failure to have repeat people logged on is the #1 reason most web sites fail. Failing sites just don't have any traffic, and many of the ones that do have traffic don't know how to manage it. As soon as a company can generate a sufficient amount of traffic, it must find ways to turn those visitors into profits.

This important transformation of visitors into buyers can be initially accomplished by either initially paying for advertising space from other high traffic sites or devising an effective plan to generate the traffic themselves. There are a number of ways to bring traffic to your web site. I will explain some of those unique ways throughout this book.

A lot of people, for some reason, think that they simply have to find the best web site designer in the business, pay them a lot of money to build a beautiful web site, and the design will then make them rich. In fact, the opposite almost always happens. Most web sites barely break even. I have seen many companies that have spent tens of thousands of dollars building a state of the art web site with all the bells and whistles. What a waste of time and money as they soon discover. If you cannot attract the traffic and keep the people coming back, you are literally wasting your time and energy.

Principles of Business

So, now that we have some basics, we are ready to get started. We will assume that you are new, have not selected a product or service, and you want to start right away. The next chapter explains in detail some tips on what products have the best chance of being successful.

Instead of trying to explain to you how everything should work, you must understand some basic principles of business first. Once you understand the principles of how business works, you can then implement a strategic plan for your new ideas into your new web business.

What is E-Commerce?

Basically, e-commerce is where people exchange products and services for money electronically over the Internet. This exchange can be done automatically, semi-automatically, or manually. If your e-commerce is done automatically, you will need to have a credit card processing machine on your web site to automatically charge your customer's credit card the exact second in time the customer's order is placed. There are some problems with this type of credit card processing, especially if you cannot deliver the product the instant it is automatically charged.

The basic rule for charging a customer's credit card is to charge it, if and only if, the product is ready to ship. If you try to charge a customer's credit card and wait until the is money deposited into your business bank account, you may find yourself in hot water with your merchant company because it is illegal! The credit card merchant companies do check on merchants from time to time, so your best bet would be to follow the rules.

If exchange is done semi-automatically, you will have to have a secure on-line shopping cart that allows the customer to browse your web site and add various items to a shopping cart; then, when they are finished, they would check out the order through your secure encrypted server. You would receive the customer's order via a secure module, and you would actually key in the customer's credit card information on your own processing equipment or via a secure on-line merchant account when the merchandise has been shipped.

When you buy something at the local convenience store or the local mall, you are participating in commerce. If you buy something online through a web site, you are participating in e-commerce. Both are forms of commerce; however, with e-commerce, the operating expenses are far less costly, and the profit margins are many times higher.

When you think about e-commerce as we have just described it, you can easily relate it to the people involved. These people are described below:

Buyers - are the people that are interested in your product or service and want to purchase it. They would place orders on-line.

Sellers / Dealers - are the people with the product or services you are looking for and the people who actually sell the product or service to you. If you intend to operate your own e-commerce web site, you would be considered the seller.

Distributors - are the people that are similar to the sellers and can actually be dealers as well. However, they purchase the product at a discounted rate from the people that make the product. If they only sell to dealers in different locations and not to consumers, they can be called distributors.

When distributors raise the price and resell the product to the consumers directly, they can be considered dealers as well. Basically, a distributor is a middle person that distributes the product one way or another.

Manufacturers - Manufacturers are the people that create the products that are sold, at a discounted price, to the dealers and distributors. They can afford to sell this way because some manufacturers have hundreds and even thousands of dealers and distributors around the world that do all the advertising and marketing for them. Most people think that the manufacturers make the highest profit margin, but most of the time, it is the dealers who actually do. However, if a manufacturer sells the product directly to the consumer, the profit margins are huge. This has not traditionally happened very often, but it is happening more often all the time because the dealers are driving the manufacturers' prices down because they are discounting the prices on the Internet.

Over the years, I have seen manufacturers step in and not allow the dealers to discount their products on the Internet. As the dealers continue to drive down the prices of the products, I expect this trend to increase vigorously over the next few years.

Analyze the Elements

When you analyze all the elements of e-commerce and how it works, it can be quite complicated, especially when you begin to learn about all the fine points in the process. Basically, when a visitor comes to your web site, it's pretty plain and simple. You want the visitor to buy something from your company, and you want them to pay for it using a form of credit purchase, like a credit card.

A typical scenario would be that a visitor would find your web site through some type of marketing tool or by using one of the many search engines on the Internet. After they find your web site, they would then "browse" or look through all your information. Next, when they find something they are interested in, you want them to place it in their secure on-line shopping cart. A secure on-line shopping cart is a digital program that remembers what the user has selected and places it in a temporary file until the user decides to order the product(s) or cancel the cart and move on to a "better" company.

If the customer decides to go ahead and purchase the product from you, he/she goes to a special area that the shopping cart has remembered and types in their name, address, telephone number, credit card information, and other information that you determine. Whenever the customer fills out all of the information requested, they click on a Submit Order icon, and the order is automatically processed and sent to you via some sort of secure way of transportation. After you receive it, you would enter it into your accounting software and process the order.

Wouldn't it be great if every web site business was that easy and every person visiting your web site purchased something? That is far from the truth. As a matter of fact, you may have hundreds or even thousands of visitors visiting your web site before you even make one sale.

Keep Customers Coming Back

You need to figure out a way to get people to not just come to your web site. You need to find a way to keep them coming back at least once a week. This process of getting people to return to your place of business is called e-commerce marketing. If no one knows that your on-line store exists, you will never sell anything; and if you cannot get a person to return more than once to your online store, you are wasting your time and money in your marketing.

Let's use your local mall as an example. Okay. There is a mall in a city with a population of fifty thousand. Let's say that your local mall receives five thousand visitors a day. Now, if everyone in this small town of fifty thousand only goes to the mall once throughout his or her entire life, then the mall would have virtually no more visitors after just ten days! The mall relies on people returning many times each year. Your e-commerce web site should rely on the same concept in order to be successful.

Accepting On-Line Payments

Different types of businesses rely on different ways to accept payment for a product or service. Retail stores, such as K-Mart®, Wal-Mart®, JC Penney®, and Sears® use various forms of accepting payment for their products and services. They have checkout stations where people stand in line and wait to pay for their merchandise. You can normally use cash, credit cards, checks, or, in some cases, you can even put down a small deposit and place an item on layaway.

Fast food chains, however, normally only accept cash as a form of payment for the meals you purchase. Fast food chains normally do not accept major credit cards for payment for a number of reasons. It is very inconvenient because of how many transactions happen in a day's time. Fast food chains rely on selling large amounts of food to make a profit. If they started accepting credit cards, they would be responsible for large transaction fees in addition to charge backs they might have.

When a customer complains about a tangible product for which they received a charge on his or her credit card statement, a charge back (credit) occurs. In other words, if you bought something and did not receive the complete product, or it was just not what it was claimed to be, you can request a refund through the merchant account that authorized the credit card. The company you purchased the product from would have to reimburse you for the charge.

Have you ever driven through the drive-through at a fast food chain and ordered something only to find when you arrived home that part of your order was missing? Of course you have. Imagine thousands of people calling the credit card company of your favorite fast food chain and requesting charge backs for the items they did not receive such as fifty-nine cent French fries. Normally the missing products would be less than a few dollars per item and would cause a nightmare for any accountant for these fast food restaurants. That's why credit card charges are simply not done for fast food purchases.

On the other hand, your Internet web business, for obvious reasons, cannot accept cash as payment. Credit cards are the standard payment option for most e-commerce businesses.

An E-Commerce Summary Checklist

The checklist below describes various things we have discussed that you should do in order to operate an e-commerce business properly and profitably.

A Great Business Idea. If you do not have something that is unique, marketable, and profitable, you will not go very far. You may as well thank me now for only spending the price of this book. However, we have dedicated a complete chapter later on to assist you with product selection criteria so that you can find the unique, marketable and profitable product that's just right for you and your business.

Business License. Consult the business license section located in your local Yellow Pages. You will need this license to acquire a Business Tax Identification number that will allow you to open a business checking account.

Business Checking Account. In order to accept credit cards from a merchant, you will need to have a business checking account.

Merchant Account. You need a bank or financial service company that will allow you to accept credit card orders.

Marketing Plan. You need a plan that states exactly what you want to accomplish. We have a whole section on this topic in a later chapter.

Product or service. THIS is what you are going to sell!

Web Site. This is your store where you are going to sell your product or service.

Customers. You need a marketing plan to get patrons to come into your on-line store and purchase your products or services. Some might call customers a business' most valuable resource.

Shopping Cart. The on-line program that allows the potential customer to "browse" your on-line store and select items, placing them in an electronic shopping basket until you "Check Out" the order for them.

Facility. A physical location where you would work and fulfill your customers' orders.

The above checklist is very simple yet practical. Try not to expect too much too fast. If you follow some basic fundamental guidelines, you are already halfway there.

Chapter 3

Selecting a Successful Product or Service

Selecting the Right Business

There is no magic formula for selecting the right product, service, or business. However, there are some guidelines you can follow from the start that can give you an incredible advantage over the competition. The first thing you should do before you even start your new business is to love and enjoy the business you are about to get into.

By doing something that you are very interested in and not doing it for the money, your chances of success are several times greater. Let's face it. Nobody wants to be stuck doing something they do not enjoy. That's why people start a business in the first place, because they hate what they do and do not want to work for anyone else. Try to think real hard about that before you jump into anything.

Take Your Time

If you want to start an on-line Internet company, the first thing you should do is to plan on spending several days—even weeks—doing keyword searches on everything you can think of that you find interesting. Take out a pen and a piece of paper and write down every single word or topic you did research on. You may spend a whole day researching just a few products.

Go to the different search engines and key in "Keyword" searches that relate to the business you are interested in starting. Make a note on what type of business you are doing research. Make lots of notes on all the competition you find—companies or organizations that relate to your searches.

This step is very important, and you do not want to miss anything. You will find out later why you are doing so much research. If you are going to spend the rest of your life running your own business, it won't hurt to spend a few weeks researching everything you can—including the competition. There are even ways that you can determine approximately how much Internet traffic your competitors actually receive. This is a point we will go over in detail in the "Marketing Your Web Site Section" later in this book.

A lot of people come up with wild crazy ideas in their heads, and they think they have the perfect product. They think they can spend five or ten thousand dollars of their savings on an Internet web site, and the money will just start rolling in. If that is what you think, then you might as well start looking for another career before you even waste one day on your idea.

To successfully operate a profitable Internet web presence, you must love what you do and you must be willing to dedicate as much time as it takes to meet your expectations and make the presence successful. I can't count how many 80-hour weeks I have worked to arrive where I am now. Many years later, I still find myself up at three o'clock in the morning just thinking about new ideas and ways to always keep ahead of the competition.

"If you are going to spend the rest of your life running your own business, it won't hurt to spend a few weeks researching everything you can including the competition."

Realistic Product Options - Eliminating Bad Internet E-Commerce Ideas

Now that we have talked about e-commerce, what it is, and some fundamental ideas on how an on-line Internet business should be run, it is time to start eliminating some "Bad E-Commerce Ideas" that may be running through your head. I call them exactly what they are: "Bad E-Commerce Ideas." That does not mean that they are bad business ideas. It only means that your chances of earning a living from certain ideas are so low that you could actually make more money mowing lawns than you could with some of them.

Let's take Pete for example. Pete is a hard-working man who wants to start an Internet business. Pete loves a challenge and can make any business work in a hometown retail sector. Pete makes baseball caps for all the local youth baseball players in his hometown. Pete has this crazy idea that he wants to open up an Internet business and sell his custom made caps on the net. His hats each take about five dollars to make, and he sells them for ten dollars a piece in his local town.

This profit margin is great in his hometown where Pete can deliver the caps himself to the hundreds of people that buy his product every week. However, on the Internet, his profit margin is not that great at all. In fact, it is terrible! Pete just spent about five thousand dollars making one of the flashiest sites I have seen. You know, the ones I find quite annoying. He was following some good marketing guidelines, and he was seeing about two hundred visitors a day to his web site. Still, he had to lower his price to seven dollars a cap because of competition on the Internet.

Remember the research you did before you were supposed to start your business? Well, this is where your pricing comes into play. Out of the two hundred potential customers visiting his web site per day, only about four were giving Pete orders. It was costing him about five dollars a cap, and he was selling each for seven dollars. In addition, Pete was paying about one dollar to ship each cap out the door. His costs did not even include the time he had invested in the whole operation.

So, if Pete has sunk five thousand dollars into his flashy web site, and he is selling four caps a day, he is making less than one dollar per cap before the credit card merchant company takes its cut as well.

You can clearly see that Pete is not a bad businessperson. He is actually doing very well if he is receiving four orders a day, but he jumped into the wrong market! Imagine if Pete were in a market where his profit margin was two hundred dollars per product instead of one dollar? He would be making eight hundred dollars a day instead of only four. I think you can see why Pete is ready to close down his Internet hat business and start working overtime to pay for his bad investment.

Mayra started her Internet business at the same time Pete did. The only difference was that Mayra only paid about one thousand dollars for her web site (four thousand dollars less than Pete) and selected a different product from the research assignment I gave her. Mayra then took the remaining four thousand dollars and invested in the right places on the Internet for marketing. Four thousand dollars can go a long way when you first get started—if you know exactly where to put it!

Instead of selling baseball caps for seven dollars each, Mayra was selling a high profit margin collectible product for three hundred dollars, and she was getting "Keystone" for her product because of its collectibility. ("Keystone" is purchasing something for a certain amount, such as one hundred and fifty dollars, and selling it for double that amount or three hundred dollars.) She was making one hundred and fifty dollars every time she sold one product, and she was selling about four items every day, just like Pete!

So, from these small examples, you can see how important the product selection criteria are to your business. While Pete and Mayra both started businesses at the same time and were seeing about the same amount of web traffic every day, Pete just jumped in without doing any research. He based his Internet business on his proven hometown enterprise and was making four dollars a day profit.

Mayra, on the other hand, did the two weeks of required research I suggested to her. She already knew the competition before she started and was able to make about six hundred dollars a day profit! I don't know about you, but I would surely rather make six hundred dollars a day as opposed to only four dollars.

David Hawkins, one my first clients, owned a health food retail store. David is an herbalist who has only been sick about two times in his entire life. When I went to meet him for the first time, I remember walking through his health food store, glancing at all the products on the shelves, and when I walked into his office, I found him lying down on his sofa—as sick as can be.

I avoid shaking hands with sick people because, of course, it is the easiest way to spread germs. I believe I shook his hand anyway, and we started talking about doing a web site for his business. Since I had been referred to him and was one of the few people doing that kind of work in the area, he agreed to let me build his on-line e-commerce web site.

The man had thousands of health food products on his shelves, so I knew I would probably not be making much of a profit on this job. But he was my second client, and every step counts when you're building a list of satisfied customers, so I would do what it took to make his web site run smoothly.

After about three weeks of taking pictures of his mainstream products and incorporating them into his new online business, we were just about ready. It was much easier getting a good registration at that time, and there was hardly any competition as well, so it went through flawlessly.

Within about two weeks, David started getting orders through his secure e-mail connection; his e-commerce business was starting to move along very quickly. After being on the Internet for about two months, he was receiving about ten orders a day, which was very good.

His average product price was about sixteen dollars, and he was selling for "Keystone," so he was making about eight dollars on each item sold. By selling ten products a day at eight dollars profit for each, David was making about eighty dollars a day profit on his Web Site, or about twenty-nine thousand two hundred dollars a year.

In order to keep his e-commerce business operating smoothly and his orders going out the door on time, he had to hire a special person to process the orders and take care of all service with the new customers.

With everything it takes to successfully operate a profitable web site such as marketing, staff, inventory, shipping, returns, taxes, credit card processing fees, and all miscellaneous expenses, his web site never once broke even.

Even though David is a very successful businessperson who makes more than one million dollars a year in his retail store, his type of business is not really a good choice for e-commerce profitability. It is good as an advertising and marketing tool, however, so if you plan on making a career on selling herbal products on the Internet, you may want to reconsider your options.

Avoid Small Ticket Items

Sometimes consumers like to shop in a local environment the hometown way. These types of custom small ticket items are good hometown businesses because of the loyal customers that will be with you for many years to come. However, on the Internet, there are new e-commerce stores popping up every day, and it changes your competition almost monthly.

Imagine having a retail store in which you sell a certain product, and every month, another businessperson builds another store right there in your neighborhood. Every one of them is selling the identical products you do. Every month! That is exactly what happens on the Internet.

Try to avoid small ticket items if at all possible. There are certain cases where small ticket items can be very successful, but you must have large amounts of established traffic already in place, and you must be an expert in Internet marketing to pull it off.

The best advice to remember when you are first starting out is—if you cannot sell something for "Keystone" and/or at least fifty dollars profit per sale, your chances of success on the Internet are very slim. By sticking to this "Keystone" and no small ticket concept, about seventy percent of all Internet ideas have just been eliminated. The larger the profit margin, the better your chance of success.

The following scenario really happened. As a matter of fact, I have seen the same thing happen dozens of times with different companies and products. You can see that there are many different ways to select the right product for your new Internet Company. Try not to select the wrong one from the beginning.

"Part of my success has come from teaching companies how to sell the same thing in a different way, while doubling their business at the same time."

Before you start that new business, remember to try to find that big-ticket item if at all possible. If you are going to sell anything on your web site, remember that it is much better to make one hundred dollars per sale opposed to only two or three dollars.

Just imagine someone starting an on-line business where you can sell something like replica Lamborghini's, Jaguars, or Ferraris for forty-five thousand dollars and it only cost you twenty thousand dollars to purchase them. Of course, this is just an example, but it is possible. The profits would be so unbelievable that you would only have to sell one or two items per month to make a good living. If you can get the traffic in the form of visitors and keep them, you are guaranteed a pretty good return on your investment.

Selling a Product with Minimum Quantities

The reason a company would sell a product with minimum quantities would be that the product would not make enough money if it were sold as a single unit. Let me give you a real example. I had a client come to me wanting to start a new Internet business, but she had no idea where to start. I asked her a series of questions and found out that she was interested in the medical field.

One would think that someone interested in the medical field would have no chance on the Internet at all because how could anyone help someone they are never able to see? I did my routine marketing analysis and started doing "Key Word" searches on everything I could think of in the medical field. What I found was very interesting. I went to one of the Pay-Per-Click services and used their search term suggestion tools to see exactly how many people were actually keying in certain words. I used many different combinations of words and wrote down exactly how many people were actually keying in each set of words. For my first test I used the words, "Drug Testing."

Next, I went to the main Pay-Per-Click Search Engine and keyed in the same words "Drug Testing" and clicked on Search. Basically, what this did was to give me a detailed idea of what was really going on. It showed me that about 30,000 people were doing key word searches for the words "Drug Testing" every month in this one particular search engine.

In addition, at the time, there was no competition at all. There were a few web sites that used pay advertising to be found using these two words. What that showed me is that there was a market for drug testing products. It also gave me an idea of how many people keyed the same thing in all the other search engines.

If 30,000 people a month were keying in "Drug Testing" in this one search engine, I would expect that a ratio of visitors per actual key word searches for "Drug Testing" could be predicted with any of the other large search engines. Basically, all I needed to know was the total number of people who visited each individual search engine every month, and I could multiply that number by the percentage I received from the Pay–Per-Click Web Site. It is basic math, but hardly anyone does it.

PPC=Pay Per Click   SE=Search Engine

Traffic Prediction	PPC SE	SE 1	SE 2	SE 3
Total Visitors Per Month	5,000,000	27,000,000	50,000,000	8,000,000
Multiplied by Percentage	.006%	.006%	.006%	.006%
Total People Searching	30,000	162,000	300,000	48,000

Note: By entering the numbers you already know; you can actually predict an approximate number of people that search for those particular words.

Any new web site coming on board would be crazy not to see what it is up against. Imagine knowing how much traffic you will receive and exactly how much it will cost before you even build your web site! What an advantage you would have!

That is the type of planning I have taught many companies to do. By doing this research, you are not only staying ahead of your competition, but they won't even know what happened until you already have so much cash flow, it wouldn't make any difference. One of the strengths you can develop from reading this book is the way you analyze and take apart the process and use the system to benefit your new business. In other words – Make Money!

Now that we had determined what product she would sell, we had to figure out how we were going to sell it. We found a manufacturer that would allow her to sell its product with only a minimum order placed every month. These drug-testing kits sold for about twenty dollars. They were FDA cleared, so any large company or corporation could use them to test their employees for various drugs at any time.

Instead of selling each drug testing kit for $20, we decided to place a minimum of five instead on individual single orders. By requiring the placing of a minimum order, we had just raised our "minimum " order received from $20 to $100.

To go a step further, we discounted the kits. If a single company ordered 50 units, they could purchase them for $18, 100 units for $16, and so on. What happened was that many companies were placing large quantity orders of one hundred or more units within the first two months!

Now we have a brand new startup company making thirty thousand dollars in its third month of operation. Some companies don't make that much money on the Internet in a whole year. Because we took all the "right" steps and covered every base possible to make the business a success, it was!

This case study is just a small example of how easy it is to get into something that can make huge profits very quickly. The only thing I did for that business that was different than what I would do for any other business when they first go on the Internet was about two full weeks of research to determine what the outcome would be before I even started.

Outsmart the Competition

It amazes me how so many good on-line businesses miss out on something so very important. Part of my success has come from teaching companies how to sell the same thing in a different way while doubling their business at the same time. I call this "Outsmarting the Compe-tition."

Let's take, for example, a CD duplication company for which I consulted. This CD company had its own web site and was doing pretty well on the Internet. CD duplication is mass duplicating information such as music, video, audio, Internet programs, etc… on a CD-ROM. Even though the company could duplicate one CD for around a dollar, they had a minimum order of 100 or a sale of one hundred dollars or more for each client. If we go to the minimum profit margin requirements we discussed earlier, it appears that it would not be feasible to get into a CD type of business. However, after doing your research, you will find that most customers do not order just one item. Most of the time, in fact, they order in increments of five hundred, a thousand, ten thousand or even more. You can see how a single sale can add up to huge profits very quickly.

This company's head person had a small office in his home. The company grossed a few hundred thousand dollars a year and received about one hundred hits (visitors to their web site) each day. The company approached me via a referral and asked if there was anything I could do for them. I carefully analyzed their web business and devised a preliminary marketing plan that would not only double their sales but also triple their profits. The company would actually still be doing the same thing, just a little differently.

The first thing I did was to analyze everything the company did in their business and then study the competition. I found that the competition, at the time, was not that bad. They also sold a few CD-R's in their CD duplication business. CD-R's are recordable CD-ROMS. The profit margins for the CD-R category were not that high, but then I noticed that there was literally no competition in that sector. By doing my research, I realized that just as many people were looking for CD-R's as were looking for CD-Duplications.

I explained to the company heads that I would market their existing web site by placing a good listing for them in the major search engines that would double their traffic. In addition, I recommended that the company completely design a web site that specialized in CD-R's and listed CD-Duplication in the site description. After two months of work, everything began to fall into place just as I had planned. The end result was two web sites specializing in both product lines but actually registered on the Internet in two different ways.

Instead of drawing one hundred visitors to their web site every day, the CD-Company now received more than two hundred new visitors logging onto the main site daily. In addition, the new CD-R web site was registered and marketed so it would be at the top of most search results. As a result, the CD-R web site received about two hundred new visitors a day, and now, all product lines were available through both sites, which tripled their profits. (In a later chapter, I will explain, in detail, some marketing tips that raised these companies to the top of most search results.)

So, after two months of restructuring this business and creating an additional web site, the results were very positive. Their main business had doubled its site traffic and sales, and the additional business I set up for them was grossing as much as the 1st business had before I met them just a few months earlier.

How could this happen? Was there some kind of secret here? No. The answer is quite simple. We simply outsmarted the competition and positioned the company to be three times as strong. After just a few months, this company moved from a crowded home office to a beautiful 1,500 square foot suite, hired two additional staff members, and tripled their sales figures. They did almost one million dollars in sales the year I helped them. This company did not sell anything different or unusual. They sold the same thing in a different way, outsmarted their competition, and tripled their sales. Of course, this story is just a brief description of everything that happened. You can easily visualize how possible this kind of success really is for your business.

Unique Markets

Another small example of how you can outsmart the competition can be seen in the case of the lingerie company for which I consulted several years ago. At the time, there were only a handful of businesses that sold lingerie on-line, but today, there are literally hundreds of lingerie web sites on the Internet. It is very easy to become a dealer—perhaps too easy. A woman came to me and asked me if I could help her out with her on-line lingerie business. She said, "I used to do very well. However, new lingerie web sites are popping up every day, and they all are naming their on-line businesses to include the letter "A" and "numbers" that place them at the top of any search results. This change puts me farther and farther down on the list, and I make fewer sales every month."

It would appear, at first glance, that her market was just too saturated, and businesses don't really make that much profit in that sector in good times. I started asking her a few questions: "What are the ten most expensive items you sell?" As she started listing off a few items, I noticed she said "corsets." I had heard of corsets, but I never really knew that much about them.

That night, I went to my computer and started

researching the list she had given me. I noticed something very remarkable that the hundreds of the other lingerie web sites had missed. There were only four competitors selling corsets, and the average price was between one hundred fifty and four hundred dollars. The corsets were such a unique product that more than 100,000 keyword searches were done every month on "corsets," and only four companies that sold them appeared in the search results.

I suggested that she purchase another domain name (Internet address) and register it as a corset company. Then she should give the web business a name that started with the letter "A," like "Affordable" or "Absolute" Corsets. That way, after registration, her company would come up in search engines as one of the top listings. Now the company has two web sites specializing in two different products.

This person always sold one type of product; however, by researching the market for a custom product and starting a separate web business for that particular product alone, she doubled her site traffic. In addition, the company actually had more in sales on the "custom" product than they did in their original business. And just think… the change only took a couple months, and there was the success they wanted and needed.

Another unique market idea could be something new or improved. When I first moved to Jacksonville Florida many years ago, I immediately retained a small office about ten minutes from the downtown area. It did not take long to make new business contacts and acquaintances. One new colleague was the man that worked down the hallway who owned a vinyl siding company.

James and I became immediate friends, and after about six months as "working neighbors," we decided to put together a vinyl siding web site for his business. Even though I mentioned to him that most small town businesses really couldn't make a substantial profit on the Internet, we decided to take a shot at it anyway.

We built him a moderately conservative web site and started to use my search engine registration techniques to register it on the Internet. We did not try registering the site on a national or international level. Instead, we registered it as a "Vinyl Siding" company in "Jacksonville, Florida." In a later chapter, you will find a detailed description of exactly how to register your web site the correct way.

By registering his vinyl siding company in a local directory instead of a standard business category, someone in Jacksonville would get a direct hit on his web site when keying in "vinyl siding. It is specific to his area of business.

His web site was certainly not something that made him enough money to retire, but I believe that, over the first six months in business, it drew in about five to ten thousand dollars in sales. Because the vinyl siding business involves about seventy percent materials and labor, the profit margins were pretty low.

It is best to completely evaluate what type of business you are about to enter in on the Internet. Even though it may be a type of business that is very profitable in a local environment that does not necessarily mean it will be profitable on the Internet. Try to do as much research as possible, and completely evaluate every possible advantage and disadvantage of the business you would like to get into. By studying every possible avenue, you are eliminating failure and setting yourself up for success!

Selecting a Product or Service Summary Checklist

The checklist below describes various things we have discussed in selecting the right product for your business. Consider this list when deciding your choice.

Love and enjoy the business you are about to get into. You do not want to be stuck doing something you dislike no matter how much money you make.

Research. Spend at least a few weeks researching your business, competition, and marketing plan. Keystone and $50 profit or more/avoid small ticket items. If you cannot sell something for "Keystone" and/or at least $50 profit per sale, your chances of success on the Internet are very slim. The larger the profit margin, the better chance of success.

Uniqueness. Find a truly unique product or service that you can offer.

Specialize in something with not much competition.

Outsmart the competition. Find ways to sell the same thing in a different way, doubling your traffic and business at the same time.

Name your business effectively. Try to name your Internet Business with either a word beginning with an "A," "B," or "C" or a number as they almost always come up first in the Search Engines. Internet businesses that start with the letters "X," "Y," or "Z" almost always come up last in a keyword search unless they pay for some additional service advertising.

Chapter 4

Your Keys to Success

Valuable Keys to Real Success

1) **"Surround yourself with positive/loyal people you can trust."** By surrounding yourself with positive and loyal people you can trust, you are greatly increasing your chances of success.

2) **"Create a business/marketing plan."** Create a business/marketing plan and try to stick with it.

3) **"Manage your cash flow with care."** Cash flow is the main source of energy behind every business.

4) **"Manage a subscription mailing list."** This is the equivalent of having flood insurance.

Loyalty and Trust

Surround yourself with positive people. Find the best people to do specific jobs and pay them what they are worth. The quicker you eliminate the negativity in your life and learn that you are in complete control of your life and where you are heading, the better off you will be. It is amazing how a company can have so little and grow so fast just by surrounding themselves by positive, high energy, qualified people who know what they want out of life.

> **"Make a list of all the negative people in your life who try to bring you down, and stay as far away from them as you can."**

Make sure your spouse supports everything you do because you are going to need him or her. Business is tough enough. Business on the Internet can be even tougher if you don't take the correct steps and have a good support system. People who say, "That idea will never work" or "you will never be able to make that business work", are people you do not need in your life. Make a list of all the negative people in your life who try to bring you down, and stay as far away from them as you can.

Over the many years I have been in business, I have learned one very important lesson. Find someone you can trust who can do a good job and stick with that person. Be up front and honest about everything, and you will not go wrong. Be honest to yourself, and trust in God to help you through difficult times.

Whenever a new Internet web company is formed, there is usually a group of people that know the inside scoop — all the best ways to make a company a success. That group could include a marketing agent, salesperson, an owner, and a web developer — just about anyone. If you are fortunate enough to have these people in your life and business, make a commitment to them as long as they give you and your ideas 100%. Of course, these people should take an active role in the continuing success of your business and have specific job duties every month.

A perfect example of how a loyal business relationship can benefit your company can be described in a real life example. I have this kind of bond with a dear friend and colleague of mine.

Many years ago I was visiting an attorney friend of mine and explained to him what I did for a living. Our business meeting did not have anything to do with my company, but he said to me, "You really need to meet this friend of mine, Lloyd Middleton. This man has been struggling with his Internet business, and I believe you can benefit him." A few minutes later, he gave me Middleton's telephone number and said I should give him a call.

About three or four days later, I saw his telephone number on my desk and decided to give him a call. I started by saying, "Hi Lloyd. My name is Robert, and your friend said you may be able to utilize my services." As I explained to him what I did, he became excited about meeting me. Our very first telephone conversation lasted about forty-five minutes, so I knew that this was a very nice man who really liked to talk, just as I do. I honestly did not believe that anyone could have more to say than I ever have, but Lloyd sure did talk a lot.

About a week later, I met with Lloyd at his office, and we hit it off right from the start. At that time, I was not as knowledgeable as I am now, but I still was bright enough to know that I could help him out. I completed my proposed projects with him, and he paid me for those services. We were both very happy in our business relationship for the first three years. He had a few Internet sales each month, which totaled a few hundred dollars, and I was receiving my $100 monthly server fee and updating fees and keeping an eye on his web site.

Over the years, Lloyd generated about twenty orders or so in sales a month, and our business relationship remained a very good one. Lloyd and I became good friends as well. It wasn't until about the late 1990s that I decided to change the whole way I operated my business — a huge risk on my part. Lloyd was the very first client I was going to approach about my new concept on how our businesses could work much better for both of us. I trusted Lloyd. I knew his response to my "concept" or "proposal" would probably determine the success of my new vision.

It was January when I finally had enough courage to call Lloyd and declare, "Lloyd, my business is just not working out as good as it used to. Every time I make a company a success, it turns around and drops my monthly service contract because it can find cheaper site hosting almost anywhere. They became greedy. They forget about all the money I've made them. My services are no longer needed because the companies got what they wanted, and now they think that they do not need me any more."

Lloyd paused for a second and took a deep breath. "I know exactly what you mean," he said. "It happens to me all the time too! Not only with employees, but with dealers as well." He then told me about all the people and companies that he had helped from ground zero in the manufacturing process only to have them turn around and abandon him.

"People get greedy and forget exactly where they come from." He then asked me, "What exactly do you have in mind about doing business differently?" Now came the hard part. I replied, "I want to make more money, but I want to really earn it."

I started to talk. "Lloyd, I want you to think about this before you give me an answer. I have been doing some research for several months now, and I believe I have devised a way where we can both make a lot more money and never have to ever worry about anyone giving us the shaft again. I will never charge you a monthly server fee again. I will never charge you for any web site updates again. Anytime you want something done, I will do it at no charge. You know that big job I just did for you for about five thousand dollars? You can keep it. All I want is a small percentage of your Internet business. Better yet, I will get rid of almost all of my existing clients and work exclusively with you."

I went on. "Give me 15% of your Internet business, and I will do whatever it takes to make your company a success." Remember, this was the first time I had ever approached anyone with my concept. You can imagine how nervous I was. Lloyd paused for a second and said, "Let me talk about it to my wife, and I will get back with you in a few days after I go through some numbers." I thought, "Lloyd is a brilliant man, and I know if he does the math, he will realize that this idea will benefit him greatly."

A few days later, Lloyd called me back and said, "Robert, I believe we can do business. We are currently selling about a few thousand dollars a month on our web site, but what we have to remember is that, since I am the manufacturer, every time I sell a product to a dealer, we make about twenty dollars profit. Every time we sell a product on the Internet, we make five times that amount because we do not have to wholesale the product to the dealers." So, basically every time we sold a product on the web site, it would be like selling five items to a dealer. That's five times the profit! After giving me my 15% off the top, Lloyd was still making over a hundred dollars per product as opposed to the twenty he was making through his dealers. What a deal!

This new business relationship not only benefits both of us, but if I slack off during any particular month, my commission checks slack as well. This concept is an "earn as much as you're worth, but you have to earn it" philosophy. I told Lloyd, "Trust me on this idea, and I will take your company close to $1,000,000 in sales in 365 days! We implement my marketing plan and strategies, and you support me 100%, and by the end of the 365th day, our sales figures will be higher than you can imagine! " Now if you start here to figure out the math, you may realize that 15% of $1,000,000 is $150,000. That amount may seem like a lot of money to pay someone to run his or her web site, and that was a big risk to me as well. I would have only one important client and I could pick up the rest on a few others! However, I always made over 100K anyway, and I was willing to drop most of my clients and work mostly with him. Now, if you look at the deal that way, how many of you would gamble an already established $100,000 a year salary to work with one major client only? Not many.

In addition, if I could actually pull this idea off, it would profit his company an additional $500,000 a year! What a twist of fate this endeavor could be! So, after ana- lyzing everything and agreeing on our contract, it was time to get busy!

This story is a perfect example of how loyalty, trust, and a strong faith in God work together. Lloyd is loyal to me, and I am loyal to him, we are both loyal to God. In addition, we both make more money! Not only is it good for business to be loyal, but I actually feel really good about myself as well.

Now, not only would this new concept be a corpora- tion's dream come true, it would be the consultant's dream come true as well. I do not know if you caught the numbers, but 15% of $1,000,000 is $150,000 a year for the consult- ant. That would mean a raise for me!

One hundred and fifty thousand dollars is a lot of money to pay to a consultant. However, this particular one hundred and fifty thousand dollars commission will actually earn the corporations an extra five hundred thousand dollars a year in profit! That's some serious cash, considering it was never there for the corporations before now. It did not take long for Lloyd to agree to my proposal, and that's how I started my first single client project. The only thing I had to do was generate a $1,000,000 in sales with Lloyd and only a handful of other clients, something which came naturally to me.

Create a Business/Marketing Plan

There are numerous ways to put together a good business or marketing plan. The plan really does not have to be technical. However, it should answer all of the questions any potential investor may bring to your attention.

Success in business depends on the results; results start with an initial plan. The plan outline should describe in detail what your ideas and goals are, why you have these ideas and goals, what problems or obstacles you have to overcome, all financial aspects of the business, and exactly what you have to do in order to obtain the end result — what you are trying to accomplish.

In a regular business, you must have a business plan if you need financing from creditors or investors. On the Internet, however, it is essential to have a combination business/marketing plan in order to succeed. With a business on the Internet, you cannot pass out flyers in your local area, make telephone calls, and stand out in the street waving a sign promoting your business. You cannot expect the same results you might get in a local business environment.

As a matter of fact, one would look and sound silly trying the same approach in an Internet-based business. Imagine having a team of telemarketers making telephone calls every day trying to tell the people they call that they are from "www dot their business name dot com." Imagine passing out flyers with that same information in your local town. It would be a complete waste of time.

"If you are in a business that caters to a specific market in a local city, your chances of making it on the Internet are so small that you would be better off shining shoes at the airport."

Because 99% of all successful Internet web sites receive their sales from cities other than where they are located, they are not operating a regular based business. It is just the opposite. If you are in a business that caters to a specific market in a local city, your chances of making it on the Internet are so small that you would be better off shining shoes at the airport. Of course, there are several markets that can cater to both.

When you begin writing your business plan, keep in mind that you are not trying to write a best selling novel. Take your time and spend at least a few weeks going over everything again and again. Your business/marketing plan should change many times before you are finished. Take your time, relax, and enjoy what you are trying to accomplish.

It is a good idea to use some sort of universal word processing program that can be opened from most computers in the world just in case you ever e-mail your plan as an attachment to someone. A few good formats would be Microsoft Word®, Word Pad, or Microsoft Works®. Word Perfect is also a good choice. Almost every computer comes equipped with one of those programs.

You can start by setting aside a separate piece of paper for each topic in the plan and titling each page with one of the subject titles located in the checklist below. Try to come up with a set of questions that take an objective overview of your goals and ideas. The more you can put on paper, the better off you will be. Try to look at the marketing plan as an "Instruction Manual on How to Operate Your Business." You can always make modifications and adjustments later.

Try to keep your marketing plan between 20 and 40 pages. I recommend making a trip to your local office supply store and picking up a business plan computer program.

Following you will find a basic outline that would work just fine for almost every business.

Elements of a Business Plan (SBA 01/02)

1. Cover sheet
2. Statement of purpose
3. Table of contents
   - I. The Business
     - A. Description of business
     - B. Marketing
     - C. Competition
     - D. Operating procedures
     - E. Personnel
     - F. Business insurance
   - II. Financial Data
     - A. Loan applications
     - B. Capital equipment and supply list
     - C. Balance sheet
     - D. Break-even analysis
     - E. Pro-forma income projections

(profit & loss statements)
   Three-year summary
   Detail by month, first year
   Detail by quarters, second
   and third years
   Assumptions upon which
   projections were based
III. Supporting Documents
   Tax returns of principals for last three years
   Personal financial statement
   (all banks have these forms)
   In the case of a franchised business,
      a copy of franchise contract and all
      supporting documents provided
      by the franchiser
   Copy of proposed lease or purchase
      agreement for building space
   Copy of licenses and other legal documents
   Copy of resumes of all principles
   Copies of letters of intent from
      suppliers, etc.

The Business Plan - What it Includes

What goes in a business plan? This is an excellent question. And it is one that many new and potential small business owners should but often times don't ask. The body of the business plan can be divided into four distinct sections:

1. The description of the business
2. The marketing plan

3. The financial management plan and

4. The management plans

Addenda to the business plan should include the executive summary, supporting documents and financial projections.

The Business Plan –
Description of the Business

In this section, provide a detailed description of your business. An excellent question to ask yourself is: "What business am I in?" In answering this question, include your products, market and services as well as a thorough description of what makes your business unique. Remember that, as you develop your business plan, you may have to modify or revise your initial questions.

The business description section is divided into three primary sections. Section 1 actually describes your business, Section 2 the product or service you will be offering and Section 3 the location of your business and why this location is desirable (if you have a franchise, some franchisers assist in site selection).

1. Business Description

When describing your business, you should generally explain the following:

1. Legalities - business form: proprietorship, partnership, and corporation. The licenses or permits you will need.

2. Business type: merchandising, manufacturing or service.

3. Define your product or service.

4. Is it a new independent business, a takeover, an expansion, a franchise?

5. Why your business will be profitable. What are the growth opportunities? Will franchising impact growth opportunities?

6. When your business will be open (days, hours)?

7. What you have learned about your kind of business from outside sources (trade suppliers, bankers, other franchise owners, franchiser, publications).

A cover sheet goes before the description. It includes the name, address and telephone number of the business and the names of all principals. In the description of your business, describe the unique aspects and how or why they will appeal to consumers. Emphasize any special features that you feel will appeal to customers and explain how and why these features are appealing.

The description of your business should clearly identify goals and objectives, and it should clarify why you are—or why you want to be—in business.

The Business Plan – Product / Service

Try to describe the benefits of your goods and services from your customers' perspective. Successful business owners know, or at least have an idea, of what their customers want or expect from them. This type of anticipation can be helpful in building customer satisfaction and loyalty. And it certainly is a good strategy for beating the competition or retaining your competitiveness. Describe:

1. What you are selling.
2. How your product or service will benefit the customer.
3. Which products/services are in demand; if there will be a steady flow of cash.
4. What is different about the product or service your business is offering.

The Business Plan - The Location

The location of your business can play a decisive role in its success or failure. Your location should be built around your customers; it should be accessible; and it should provide a sense of security. Consider these questions when addressing this section of your business plan:

1. What are your location needs?
2. What kind of space will you need?
3. Why is the area desirable? The building desirable?
4. Is it easily accessible? Is public transportation available? Is street lighting adequate?
5. Are market shifts or demographic shifts occurring?

It may be a good idea to make a checklist of questions you identify when developing your business plan. Categorize your questions, and, as you answer each question, remove it from your list.

The Business Plan - The Marketing Plan

Marketing plays a vital role in successful business ventures. How well you market your business, along with a few other considerations, will ultimately determine your degree of success or failure. The key element of a successful marketing plan is to know your customers—their likes, dislikes, and expectations. By identifying these factors, you can develop a marketing strategy that will allow you to arouse and fulfill their needs.

Identify your customers by their age, sex, income/educational level and residence. At first, target only those customers who are more likely to purchase your product or service. As your customer base expands, you may need to consider modifying the marketing plan to include other customers.

Develop a marketing plan for your business by answering these questions. (Potential franchise owners will have to use the marketing strategy the franchiser has developed.) Your marketing plan should be included in your business plan and contain answers to the questions outlined below.

1. Who are your customers? Define your target market(s).
2. Are your markets growing? Steady? Declining?
3. Is your market share growing? Steady? Declining?
4. If a franchise, how is your market segmented?
5. Are your markets large enough to expand?
6. How will you attract, hold, increase your market

share? If your business is a franchise, will the franchiser provide assistance in this area? Based on the franchiser's strategy? How will you promote your sales?

7. What pricing strategy have you devised?

The Business Plan - The Competition

Competition is a way of life. We compete for jobs, promotions, and scholarships to institutions of higher learning, in sports—and in almost every aspect of our lives. Nations compete for the consumer in the global market place as do individual business owners. Advances in technology can send the profit margins of a successful business into a tailspin causing them to plummet overnight or within a few hours. When considering these and other factors, we can conclude that business is a highly competitive, volatile arena. Because of this volatility and competitiveness, it is important to know your competitors.

Questions like these can help you:

1. Who are your five nearest direct competitors?
2. Who are your indirect competitors?
3. How are their sales: Steady? Increasing? Decreasing?
4. What have you learned from their operations? From their advertising?
5. What are their strengths and weaknesses?
6. How does their product or service differ from yours?

Start a file on each of your competitors. Keep manila

envelopes of their advertising and promotional materials and their pricing strategy techniques. Review these files periodically, determining when and how often they advertise, sponsor promotions and offer sales. Study the copy used in their advertising and promotional materials, and learn their sales strategy. For example, is their copy short? Descriptive? Catchy? Or how much do they reduce prices for sales? Using this technique can help you to understand your competitors better and how they operate their businesses.

The Business Plan - Pricing and Sales

Your pricing strategy is another marketing technique you can use to improve your overall competitiveness. Get a feel for the pricing strategy your competitors are using. That way you can determine if your prices are in line with competitors in your market area and if they are in line with industry averages.

Some of the pricing strategies are:
Retail cost and pricing
Competitive position
Pricing below competition
Pricing above competition
Price lining
Multiple pricing
Service costs and pricing (for service businesses only)
      Service components
      Material costs
      Labor costs

Overhead costs

The key to success is to have a well-planned strategy, to establish your policies and to constantly monitor prices and operating costs to ensure profits. Even in a franchise where the franchiser provides operational procedures and materials, it is a good policy to keep abreast of the changes in the marketplace because these changes can affect your competitiveness and profit margins.

The Business Plan - Advertising and Public Relations

How you advertise and promote your goods and services may make or break your business. Having a good product or service and not advertising and promoting it are like not having a business at all. Many business owners operate under the mistaken concept that the business will promote itself, and they channel money that should be used for advertising and promotions to other areas of the business. Advertising and promotions, however, is the lifeline of a business and should be treated as such.

Devise a plan that uses advertising and networking as a means to promote your business. Develop short, descriptive copy (text material) that clearly identifies your goods or services, its location and price. Use catchy phrases to arouse the interest of your readers, listeners or viewers.

In the case of a franchise, the franchiser will provide advertising and promotional materials as part of the franchise package; you may need approval to use any materials that you and your staff develop. Whether or not this is the case, as a courtesy, allow the franchiser the opportunity to review, comment on, and, if required, approve these materials before using them. Make sure the advertisements you create are consistent with the image the franchiser is trying to project. Remember—the more care and attention you devote to your marketing program, the more successful your business will be.

The Business Plan – The Management Plan

Managing a business requires more than just the desire to be your own boss. It demands dedication, persistence, the ability to make decisions and the ability to manage both employees and finances. Your management plan, along with your marketing and financial management plans, sets the foundation for and facilitates the success of your business.

Like plants and equipment, people are resources—they are, in fact, the most valuable asset a business has. You will soon discover that employees and staff will play an important role in the total operation of your business. Consequently, it's imperative that you know what skills you possess and those you lack since you will have to hire personnel to supply the latter. Additionally, it is imperative that you know how to manage and treat your employees. Make them a part of the team. Keep them informed of, and get their feedback regarding, changes. Employees often have excellent ideas that can lead to new market areas, innovations to existing products or services, or new product lines or services, which can improve your overall competitiveness.

Your management plan should answer questions such as:

How does your background/business experience help you in this business?

What are your weaknesses, and how can you compensate for them?

Who will be on the management team?

What are their strengths/weaknesses?

What are their duties?

Are these duties clearly defined?

If a franchise, what type of assistance can you expect from the franchiser?

Will this assistance be ongoing?

What are your current personnel needs?

What are your plans for hiring and training personnel?

What salaries, benefits, vacations, and holidays will you offer? If a franchise, are these issues covered in the management package the franchiser will provide?

What benefits, if any, can you afford at this point?

If a franchise, the operating procedures, manuals and materials devised by the franchiser should be included in this section of the business plan. Study these documents carefully when writing your business plan, and be sure to incorporate this material. The franchiser should assist you with managing your franchise. Take advantage of their expertise and develop a management plan that will ensure the success for your franchise and satisfy the needs and expectations of employees as well as the franchiser.

The Business Plan – The Financial Management Plan

Sound financial management is one of the best ways for your business to remain profitable and solvent. How well you manage the finances of your business is the cornerstone of every successful business venture. Each year, thousands of potentially successful businesses fail because of poor financial management. As a business owner, you will need to identify and implement policies that will lead to and ensure that you will meet your financial obligations.

To effectively manage your finances, plan a sound, realistic budget by determining the actual amount of money needed to open your business (start-up costs) and the amount needed to keep it open (operating costs). The first step to building a sound financial plan is to devise a start-up budget. Your start-up budget will usually include such one-time-only costs as major equipment, utility deposits, down payments, etc.

Checklist of Topics for your Business/Marketing Plan

Purchase an up to date business/marketing plan program at your local office supply store. Once you have completed the sections below, you can incorporate the information into your program.

Cover Sheet. A cover sheet is a sheet of paper that includes your business name, address, phone numbers, e-mail and web site addresses.

Statement of Purpose. The statement of purpose sets out and describes what you are trying to accomplish.

Table of Contents. This is an index of everything you have in your plan with page numbers referencing the material and the pages each subject can be located on.

Business Description. This is a detailed description of your business and how it is expected to work.

Market Analysis. This section includes the marketability of your product or services. If there is a market for your product or service, determine if people need it, which would buy it, why would they buy it, etc…

Competition. Provide a complete analysis of all of your competition. Do as much research as possible and try to find out as much information you can on every other business that sells anything similar to your product or service.

Management. This is a section about you and what your responsibilities are. Include everyone involved that will take an active role in your business.

Financial Records. This section consists of gathering all of your financial records, such as credit cards, savings, and business checking accounts. It would also be a good idea to have on hand a recent copy of your credit report for your records. Financial institutions will get this information on their own if you are seeking financing, and you do not want to find any unexpected surprises. Correct them first if you can.

Operating Expenses, Profit, and Losses.
Include a detailed list of all your expected operating
expenses.

Supporting Documentation. All documents that
support what you are trying to accomplish with your
business, including patents, press releases, partners and
their financial obligations, etc... should be presented in
this section.

References. Provide a list of all personal and business references, including names, addresses, and telephone numbers.

After you have completed your business plan, hire a
professional editor and typist to type the entire plan on
bond paper. Keep a file copy on a computer if you have one.
After the plan has been edited and corrected, it is ready to
be printed and published for use. If possible, print your plan
using a laser printer and quality bond paper, and print ten
copies so you have plenty to distribute and file.

Now you can sit back, relax, and feel much better
about the way you want your business to progress. You have
an actual plan detailing your strategies.

Cash Flow—What is it?

This question is perhaps the first and most important
question you must ask yourself. Most people do not even
study the question of cash flow and just jump into a project
because they think they can build a first class web site. They
know someone who is really good at it, or they have a big
company creating their web presence for them.

I have had many potential new clients come to me and ask me to set a traffic-building program for them or get their company generating some profits. Unfortunately, there are many products and services that just cannot be profitable on the Internet. Understanding the principles of cash flow is crucial in determining if your web presence will be a success or a failure.

To get you to understand exactly how this complex process works, you must first learn a few important business terms. Even though you may not realize it, one important term will determine the success of your business. It is called **"Cash Flow."** Different people can interpret cash flow in many different ways. If you think that you will start a business and start selling your products or services and are successful in selling something, everything will be just fine; think again.

A Cash Flow Case Study

Let's take me, for example. I am in a service industry, which is a pretty easy example to understand. For starters, here is a basic scenario: Let's say I did work for a particular client during the first week of January. I bid $4000 to complete this job in one week. I do my work, write out an invoice to the client, and give them 30 days to pay it. The job was a software installation at their location, and the software cost me $2,000.

Now, let's say that I completed another particular job during the same week for a client The complete job, including labor, was invoiced at $2,000. However, the job cost me

$500 in software. I completed both of these jobs in one week. You're probably thinking, "Wow, it appears that you made $6,000.00 for one week of work. That is great!"

That is true, but not really, and here's why:

In order to understand fully how cash flow really works, you must look at ALL of the above facts. Let's throw in another little twist. For the 3 weeks, I invoiced an additional $4,000 in sales. That's $10,000 in sales for one month! Sounds pretty easy, doesn't it?

Yes, I Invoiced $6,000 for one week of work, and my total "Receivables" (money owed to me) totaled $10,000. That is correct. However, let's say, for example, I had $5,000 in my business account that particular week. Now, let's say my bills for that same week totaled $3,000, including a $600/month business telephone line. If you are late on that, they will cut it off! Have you figured it out yet? This scenario provides a picture of a perfect "Cash Flow" problem.

It appears that I have $5000, in my Business account, and I have $10,000 in receivables (money owed to me), so it looks like I have about $15,000 that I can access! Seems like—but not really.

See, you are forgetting about two very important facts. First, my bills for that week came to $3,000. No problem there. I have $5,000 in my account, right? Well, those two jobs that I Invoiced for $6,000 cost me $2,500 in software up front that I had to pay myself in order to get the jobs. $5,000 minus $3,000 for bills minus $2,500 for software equals (- $500). Interesting, isn't it?

The "Real Life" truth is this: I am actually $500 in the

hole because I will not receive the $6000 I just invoiced until 45 days down the road. Even though the money previously invoiced will trickle in every week, you can see clearly how a business can get in trouble very fast.

While this actually happened to me many times over the early years, I am gaining enough experience to avoid this "Cash Flow Problem" as much as possible in the future. BUT I will tell you this fact:

"ALMOST EVERY BUSINESS, AT SOME POINT OR ANOTHER, WILL EXPERIENCE A CASH FLOW PROBLEM!"

Steps You Can Take to Stay Ahead of Your Cash Flow

Cash flow is the main source of energy behind every business. Your business, along with thousands of other businesses around the world, needs a good cash flow to stay ahead of the competition and to stay in business!

As a matter of fact, a lot of large companies or corporations are susceptible to cash flow problems because they need a lot of cash to grow and expand. At the same time, everything has to move along smoothly from day to day in order to handle any unexpected cash flow problems. Cash can flow through your hands as easily as water if you are not careful. You will need some helpful ways to maximize your cash flow and stay ahead of it.

Below are some steps you can take to keep your cash flowing:

Pay your bills on time. This will keep you from getting behind on cash flow. Try to plan for your bill payments to be received by the vendor one to three days before they are due.

Buy only what you need, and keep your inventory levels low. If your business only has 4 employees, there is no need for 10 computers. By only purchasing the supplies you need, you can save needed cash flow every month.

Make monthly telephone calls to the people that owe you money and are late on your receivables. When you are late on your telephone bill, the telephone company is the first to let you know. You should let your customers know as well.

Pay cash for as many things as you can. The easy financing of equipment and inventory can get you in serious debt very quickly.

Reduce credit card debt. Pay higher monthly payments on your credit cards to get them paid down as quickly as possible, and don't recharge except in emergencies.

Manage a Subscription Mailing List

Believe it or not, a successfully managed mailing list can mean the difference between making and breaking your business. I remember when I would get excited every time I got ready to approve a mailing list that would be sent out. I would prep for days on exactly what my mailing advertising copy would say and how to say it correctly. Then I would push the "Approve Post" icon and instantly send my message out to several thousand people all at the same time. The best part was that, every single time I did it, the list generated more than ten thousand dollars in extra sales every week! This was in addition to regular sales we generated through other marketing means.

Before I tell you how a successful mailing should be started, you must first understand what should not be done. You should not, under any circumstances EVER send unsolicited e-mail to ANYONE for ANY reason. Unsolicited e-mail is something like purchasing a mailing list with a few million e-mail addresses and trying to contact the people on it without their permission. This tactic will get your web site shut down faster than you can imagine.

Instead, you should use creative ways to try to get the e-mail addresses of the people that visit your web site. Why should you be interested in e-mail addresses of people that visit your web site? It is quite simple. These people find their way to your web site every day for a reason. They are interested in your products or services. Not only are they interested in your products and services, but almost all of them also did some work to get there. They had to key in certain search terms on one or more search engines.

Basically, it is similar to Wal-Mart® running an ad in the local newspaper on a certain product in which you are very interested. You were interested in the product Wal-Mart® advertised, and you were interested enough that you decided to make a trip to the store to check it out. When you got there, you did one of two things: you either purchased the product or you did not.

If you did purchase the product, you might also have purchased something else on your way to the checkout counter because Wal-Mart® has so much stuff that it can be hard to resist buying something else you want or need.

Even if you did not purchase the product, you still might have purchased something else on your way out.

Regardless of what you did there, Wal-Mart® got you to come into their store, and since the store is usually located close to your home, and they have many neat things at affordable prices, you will probably make a return trip at some point in time.

The Internet is similar but different. But you still have to have something the potential customer is interested in to achieve that initial visit.

The thing to remember is that these visitors were interested in what you have to offer. Imagine everyone who left a name, address, phone number, and a note that said, "Hi, I visited your On-Line store today. I am interested in your products, but I wasn't ready to make a purchase." Or "Maybe you can contact me from time to time when you have a special. It is possible that I might buy something then."

That is exactly what a good, successful, well managed, mailing list can do for your company. The list comes from visitors you can contact later to come back and buy your product.

To get started with this process, you will need access to mailing list software that can be set up for your business.

Most Internet Service Providers already have something like this installed on their servers. I would recommend picking up the telephone and calling them. Ask, "Do you have any mailing list programs that your customers can use for our business?"

If they do, tell them you want to sign up for an account. If they do not, ask if they know where to get a program you can use. More than likely, you can have a mailing list set up in just a few days.

Now that you have your mailing list set up, what do you do with it? The first thing you need to do is to put a few of your e-mail addresses and a few of your good friends' e-mail addresses on your list and experiment with the controls for several days until you have it figured out 100%. The last thing you want to do is to send "Test Messages" to people you don't really know.

After you have your list program fine tuned, you need a form on your web site that allows users that visit your web site to sign up for your mailing list.

If you receive about two hundred visitors a day to your web site, don't expect all two hundred to sign up for your mailing list. As a matter of fact, you will do well to see five or ten a day. Let's face it. How many web sites have you visited and signed up for their mailing list? I bet not very many. Now is the time to get a little creative and build that mailing list. Remember, the people that visit your Web Site should all be considered future customers.

One of the easiest ways to build a mailing list is to give something away in exchange for an e-mail address. Let's look at how you can do that.

Let's say you were selling Nascar die cast car collectibles, and you had a "Sign up for our Mailing List" form on your Home Page. Well, people might be interested in Nascar die cast cars, but would they be willing to give me their e-mail addresses? Probably not!

Now let's use the same example, but with a little twist. The same "Sign up for our Mailing List" is located on the same page. However, now there is a flashy icon that says, "Sign up for our mailing list and be automatically entered in our monthly NASCAR Die Cast Car Giveaway!" Now, I might be a little more interested.

Let's take this discussion one step further. Let's give one car away every day for two weeks and see what happens! If you run a promotion that gives away a product of interest every day for a certain time period, and you list the winners, you will accumulate a huge mailing list faster than you think. It is called "Impulse Registration" where users become excited and give you their E-mail addresses.

There are many promotional ways to increase your mailing list fast. Give something away, hold monthly contests, and provide excellent customer service. If you do these kinds of things, you are on your way to having several thousand people on your mailing list who want to be there.

Every time someone signs up for your drawings, promotions, and mailing list, add his or her e-mail address to your list. Your master list! Keep in mind that you will have several people who will want to be removed every time you run the list. Keep the list clean and up to date, and you will be on your way to a successful Internet marketing mailing list.

Chapter 5

Ways to Save Money Using the Internet

Saving Money Opposed to Spending

If you cannot find a way to make additional revenue on the Internet, you may be looking in the wrong place. There are just as many ways to save money, as there are ways to make it. Below, you will find a real life example of how easy it is for a company to make an extra one hundred thousand dollars a year without selling one thing on its web site.

It is possible for any manufacturer to be profitable on the Internet. The company need only to want to be profitable. And yet, while a manufacturer actually has a better chance of success than any retailer does, most still choose not to invest in the Internet. Why? Let's look at a real case in point.

It all started years ago when a major multi-million dollar manufacturer saw a press release from my company in the local newspaper. It was a basic article about me entitled, "Catering to His Clients' Needs." Even though I did not write the article, the author saw something in what I was doing then that even I had not seen. That's right. I actually "catered to my clients needs." In other words, if a client wanted something, I provided it. If a client had a problem, I solved it.

I believe it is much easier for an outsider to have an accurate perspective about a company's goals. I did not know anything about the company that requested to speak with me. All I knew was that they wanted to make their web presence a success. I guess that is the key word for me—success. Even though I consider myself moderately successful, I had a thing for making other companies more successful than anyone else could. If I had figured this fact out when I started, I would have been a consultant all along, but it took me many years to figure out what I could do so well.

The company that read my press release was fairly large, grossing approximately fifty million in sales a year, and they wanted to make their Internet web presence a success. However, there was one small problem. As I stood in front of about twelve senior officers and went through my presentation, the senior officer stood up and said to me, "We need help and want our Internet web site to be successful, but we absolutely cannot compete with our 600 dealers."

In other words, this manager was saying to me, "We need your help, but we cannot sell our own products." I thought about the situation for a little while and put together a series of questions to ask them. The questions I was asking were basic questions to me, but the answers gave me what I needed to know in order to determine exactly where they stood and what they wanted to accomplish.

There I was. I had been in business for just a year; I was actually learning as I was going; and suddenly, I was standing, in a slightly wrinkled suit, in front of a board of directors, faced with the question: "What can you do for our company, and why do we need you?" Believe it or not, it only took me about 30 seconds to give my reply. Even though I knew 100% that I could not help them generate new revenue for their business, I immediately focused on how, instead, I could save them money.

Most people look at business as making more money "next year." So, when you are faced with a multi-million dollar corporation and you know that you cannot sell products online successfully because doing so would compete with their dealers, there is only one way left to win their business. You say, "Here's how much can I save you!" Saving money is just as much a winning strategy as saying, "Here's how much I can make you." The bottom line is always the bottom line no matter how you look at it.

So right there, I took a deep breath and panned from left to right, looking at everyone in the board room and said with confidence, "Based on what you told me about your business, I cannot generate any new business for you."

As each one of them looked at me with a look that said, "Who is this guy? If he wants to secure this contract, is he crazy?" After about 15 seconds in which the blood went rushing through every section of my body, I took a deep breath and said, "I'm sorry. I can't make you an extra $20,000 a year or anything extra, but I can do something else. If you follow my vision and plan, I can save your company an extra $100,000 a year! That money will give you an extra $100,000 to spend on something else!"

I had noticed this company had service manuals that were updated every month, so they spent hundreds of thousands of dollars each year keeping these manuals up to date.

I suggested the company create an electronic Intranet system that would allow their hundreds of dealers to log in via a secure user ID and password and receive up-to-date access to a current operators manual.

An Intranet system is really an internal use of the Internet. Many people can interpret the word "Intranet" many different ways. Let's try to boil down the explanation of this kind of system to its most easily understood form. If a small company had a secure location on the Internet that started with "https:" and they wanted users within their organization to be able to share information, programs, e-mail, and files without anyone else on the Internet having access to their material, they would set up special software to do so. The software verifies those logging on to their web site and gives each authorized visitor access to specific areas via a user name and password. That's a small Intranet system.

By incorporating an electronic Intranet into their business practice, they would eliminate the need for any hard copy printing of their manuals. Each dealer could log in and print his or her own up-to-date manual at any time—day or night.

After I explained in full detail how such a plan was possible, it only took them five hours to retain my services for the next six months! This was my first large contract and marked the beginning of a business relationship with this company that lasted many years. Basically, every manufacturer should look for ways to save money opposed to looking for ways of making additional revenue. If you do not have the in-house resources to figure out what you can do for positive change, contract an independent consultant, such as my firm, to assist you in your needs.

This is just one small example of how hundreds of thousands of dollars can be saved every year by using the Internet and its resources.

Checklist of Topics Suitable for Saving Money

Expensive, and if you use a secure Intranet, you can have your information delivered instantly with hardly any cost at all.

E-Mail and Video Conferencing. By using these services, your business can save a lot on telephone bills and monthly postage fees.

Chapter 6

Internet Placement, Registration, and Marketing

What Exactly are the Basic Fundamentals of Internet Placement and Registration?

The very first place you should start when it comes to marketing your new web business is search engines. A search engine is a web site destination where millions of people go to find what they are looking for by keying in a few words and pressing a "Search" button.

Search engines are very disappointing as far as I am concerned, but they are all we have at this time, so we should make the best possible use of them. If you want to see a market that is unfair, search engines is where you should look.

Do you know how many companies made hundreds of thousands of dollars just because some editor sitting at a desk worded the name and description of their business a certain way? If anything about the Internet disturbs me, it is the way "Search Engines" are operated. They started out as a pretty neat concept; however, since the late 90's, the people who manage them have become very greedy and don't really care about the content that comes up during keyword searches.

Let's face it, where else in the entire world can you do a "Key Word" search for a specific well known brand name product, and the number one listing of the product you are looking for is some person working in his underwear behind a small computer in a one-bedroom apartment? The Internet search engines, that's where!

I can envision a "Smart Search Engine" someday that caters to the needs of the millions of users, not the advertisers. I also envision engines that will give you quality answers and a variety of good content results to your questions.

Also, after a search engine displays about fifty topics that relate to your inquiry and you have looked at all of them, you have the option of saving any of the topics as your personal favorites so you can choose to view the same information again at a later date. If that were the case, and the engine gave you a new set of search results every time you did a search, we wouldn't have the same web sites come up every time just because of where the editor got paid to placed them.

At the time of the publication of this book, it's almost like winning the lottery if your web site comes up in the search engines. The ones that come up in the first five results are the lottery winners because they are the ones making all the money. I can't stress enough how important it is to get your exact title and description correct so that it places among the winners. I have seen actual cases where some web sites make hundreds of thousands more each year just because of one letter in their title and description. It is absolutely unbelievable how precise the search "game" has become!

Web Access to the Latest Information

There is no guarantee to get a good search engine placement. However, there are ways you can increase your chances of being at the top. Because Internet search engines are literally changing all the time, I want you to have access to the latest information on placement. You can go to http://www.0to1million.com/ and find up-to-date information on the topics I've included by using the following activation code.

Internet Activation Code: **680102**

How Search Engines Work

The Internet is a place where there is so much information; it is very difficult to even describe what's there because it is so tremendous. With the Internet changing every day, it is impossible to tell you all the latest techniques for all the search engines. There are, however, specific guidelines that can help you provide the best registration for your web site. Use the following as guidelines, and do your own research to refine your submissions.

The first thing to remember is that almost all of the "Best Search Engines" in which you can be listed charge two hundred to three hundred dollars just to get a good listing reviewed. YOU SHOULD PAY IT! If you see any company that says they can register your web site on one thousand search engines and directories for $99, someone is really pulling a fast one on you. What the company is really saying is, "We have automatic software that sends your information to thousands of search engines at the same time, and we want to really mess up your business for $99."

Let's look at some facts. Yahoo® alone charges $299 (12/01 yahoo®.com) for businesses to use their "Business Express" program. If this one search engine charges almost $300 for a professional to review your business, I find it quite difficult to believe a company can register your business correctly in one thousand search engines for $99. Search engines that use these moderately expensive programs may claim that they are fair, but I hardly see that to be true.

All search engines work differently from each other.

When you submit your business to each one, be sure you also spend a considerable amount of time reviewing the policy of each one.

Just because you have a number one listing in a major search engine and are making tons of money a year, that does not mean you should count on it forever. Diversification is the key to success!

Below, you will find some basic information on a few search engine companies you may want to consider. This is not to say that they are the best, but it would be a good idea to give these specific areas some consideration. These three search engine destinations can actually list you in about fourteen of the top search engines including Netscape® Search, Yahoo®, AOL™ Search, Google™, Lycos®, HotBot®, DirectHit™, MSN®, AltaVista®, Juno®, Time Warner™, Prodigy™, CNN, and Excite™. In addition, hundreds of other smaller search engines will add you to their sites as well by using these larger ones.

LookSmart™, DMOZ, and Yahoo®

Getting placed on these top three places will get your web site listed in: Netscape® Search, Yahoo®, AOL™ Search, Google™, Lycos®, HotBot®, DirectHit™, MSN®, AltaVista®, Juno®, Time Warner™, Prodigy™, CNN, and Excite™. (12/01)

Looksmart (12/01 looksmart.com)

Looksmart is definitely the best Search Engine in

which to place a listing. The LookSmart Network reaches about 77% of the whole Internet. (12/01 looksmart.com) That's better than three out of four US Internet users — an incredible ratio. Looksmart reaches so many users because Looksmart directories power many of the leading portals on the Internet including MSN®, AltaVista®, Juno®, Time Warner™, Prodigy™, CNN, and Excite™. Basically, if one can succeed in placing a good listing in Looksmart, then a pretty good registration will be within the scope of the portals that utilize Looksmart's database and information.

If you go to the Looksmart Search Engine and do a keyword search for a product or service you are interested in selling and look at the results, you will see exactly what your competition is. If there are many (more than 30) listings in a category when your Keyword search comes up, then you have a lot of competition. In general, a lot of competition may mean suffering loss of sales even before you start unless your business starts with the letter A, B, or C. (Pretty unfair, but that's just the way it is.)

Next, go to the other portals that utilize LookSmart's engine, and the same Key Word Search. Note exactly what comes up. In retrospect, if there are more than thirty competitors, and the title of your business starts with the letter "W," you will be assured a listing in all of them at the bottom of the list.

If, however, your business starts with the letter "A" and there are only five competitors on the average in each search portal, and you are selling a product or service that you make you more than $100 a sale, then your chances of having a successful e-commerce site increase by 500%!

Go to Looksmart's entire partnership of web sites and document which of your competitors come up. If you see certain competitors' web sites coming up in the first to fifth positions in four of the eight Search Engines, I would strongly recommend looking at the title of their web sites and the descriptions they used to be placed in the one through five positions.

The worst thing you can do is to try to register your web site with a lot of key words that relate to your business. Remember! The Internet has been around for years now. Simply, tricks no longer work. Instead, study the title, description, and content of the sites that are placed at the top, and write a similar, but not too flashy, comparison title and description. With a little practice and exact study of your competition, you will find yourself writing your way to the top placement positions.

Rating ***** 5 Stars: The Looksmart registration fee for business is about $299 per URL, and I strongly recommend spending the money to pay this price for their services. Please note that they also have a Pay-Per-Click option that requires a $2,500 minimum monthly fee requirement. (Looksmart.com 12/01)

DMOZ - Open Directory Project

The Open Directory Project is one of the best areas to have a good listing. They, like Looksmart, have portals all over the world that utilize their data. This search engine claims to be "the largest human edited directory on the Internet" with worldwide editors constantly making it the most comprehensive directory available.

The best part about DMOZ is that it is FREE to users. The editors are volunteers as well! It is a good idea to research your competitors as I have suggested. Research in all Internet search places, and perhaps even try to become a volunteer editor in the subject area where your web site will be listed to increase your chances of being listed where you want.

The Open Directory powers the search results for popular search engines and portals: Netscape® Search, AOL™ Search, Google™, Lycos®, HotBot®, DirectHit™, and many others.

As suggested in my discussion of other Search Engines, do your research on your competitors before you submit your business for review.

Rating ***** 5 Stars: The fact that Netscape® Search, AOL™ Search, Google™, Lycos®, HotBot®, and DirectHit™ uses the dmoz.com search results gives them 5 stars. (dmoz.com 12/01)

Yahoo®

Most people think that Yahoo® is the best search engine to use to guarantee a top listing. I believe this not to be true. Yahoo® is an excellent search engine to be listed in, but over the years, they have been toughening up their requirements and procedures on which sites will be listed and where they will come up in the search results. As they have been trying to remain competitive in the business market, Yahoo® has not been doing a good enough job giving the consumers the quality results they expect to receive.

If you were to just register a web site with Yahoo®, you are leaving your business in the hands of editors. With careful planning, you can not only get a top one to five position in search results, but you can actually get some competitors removed at the same time.

Did you know that you could actually get a competitor removed from the Yahoo® search results? I can say this with confidence because I have done it many times. All you have to do is say the right thing to the right person at the right time. Look for mistakes from the search results, and send in complaints about things that appear unfair such as a company having excessive keywords coming up in the description and title. The more you study each search engine's policy, the more you can determine exactly what to say and to whom to say it.

In order to register a web site successfully, you must do two things. First, you must study each search engine; then, you must be smarter than the people that edit those particular search engines.

In order to guarantee a good registration on Yahoo®, you must understand exactly how the process works. First of all, an editor reviews every site listed. This editor is human, and he or she has complete control of where you will be listed. If you can understand how the editor is supposed to do his/her job, then all you have to do is to be smarter when submitting your information.

The very first step in successfully registering your web site is researching your competitors. In other words, perform a preliminary key word search and see exactly what comes up. In most cases, you will see a category with a few web sites listed under the category. The initial web sites that come up receive almost all the traffic from the search string. If you can achieve a position there, you have accomplished something very special. Congratulations! If not, that is okay too.

Let's say, for example, you just cannot get listed on the search results on the first page. The category that is listed is the second best listing that you can get. Now if the category listing has 100 results, and your business name starts with the letter "P," then you are wasting your time even registering your site there because you will attract hardly any traffic. Most visitors start at the top of a list and work their way down. If someone is looking for a particular product or service, and you do not come up in the initial search and you are listed at the bottom of the category results, you are doomed to failure on the Internet before you even start!

You have just had your first lesson on having a web site on the Internet. In general, if your business name starts with the letter "A," you will have about 1000% more visitors than a business that starts with the letter "S." That is true, unless of course you have an extra million dollars for advertising. We are talking about the general concepts involved in web site registration.

Now, if you want to start a business and want to see how you will do, you can actually research your product and see how much traffic you are likely to receive even before you open for business.

This task is a little more difficult, but it can be done. Let's say, for example, you wanted to sell hats and caps in your new on-line business. Let's call your new business the

"Wilson Hat Company." The very first thing you do is to perform a "Hats" key word search to find your competitors.

Go to Yahoo®, do a key word search on "hats," and see what happens. You want to know what happens when people are looking for your site. You think you may have a great product, great customer service, and have it all together, but the fact of the matter is that "Wilson Hat Company" is doomed to fail on the Internet even before it opens!

How do I know this fact? The reason is complex, but this is why. The first problem is that even if you pay Business Express's "NON REFUNDABLE" fee for reviewing your site within a week, your site will be listed at the bottom of a list of about 100 web sites that sell the same thing. By the time someone searches for your category looking for a cap or hat, they will of course start at the top of the category, visit a few sites, and usually purchase something from one of the first five listings.

You will see several listings of hat companies come up as search results, and at the top of your screen, you will see a category that has hats in it. It will be something like "Shopping > Apparel Accessories > Hats and Caps." When you click on that link, it will bring up about a hundred or more hat companies. If you registered "Wilson Hat Company," it would fall at the bottom of that long list.

There is a second reason your business is doomed to fail under this scenario. Not only are you listed at the bottom of the category list, but also your merchandise requires that you sell enormous volume. Even if you do sell a hat for $10, it is more than likely that you have put $5 into it. If you make a sale only once in a while, you only make $5 for each sale! You would have to sell 20 hats to make $100! Are you starting to see the picture why your chances of surviving this market are very slim? GOOD!

Even though Yahoo® is the most visited Search Engine in the world, at this time, despite having many millions of visitors a day it is not exactly the easiest one on which to guarantee a good listing.

Rating ***** 5 Stars: The Yahoo® business registration fee is about $299 per URL, and I strongly recommend spending the money to pay this price for their services. (Yahoo®.com 11/01) I give them 5 stars as well because they have been leaders in the industry.

Pay Per Click

Not too long ago, some companies would give you a couple of cents if a user clicked onto their banner. Nowadays, though, it is not uncommon for you, as an Internet e-commerce company, to pay up to one dollar or more per visitor you receive from specific pay per click site!

A pay-per-click option would go something like this: you deposit a few hundred to a few thousand dollars into an account with a search engine. You would then be given a control panel where you can compete with millions of other people trying to sell the same thing you are. The company that bids the largest amount would be placed at the top according to the amount they bid. As soon as a consumer clicks on your link to go to your web site, the amount that you bid to get the top position is deducted from your account until you run out of money.

This was the brilliant concept designed to get a lot of the unprofessional web sites pushed down on the list of search results because the unprofessional web sites would not pay anything for advertising. At the same time, it has allowed the rich to become richer. There are not a lot of companies that can afford to pay up to $3 or more for every visitor that comes to their web sites. This brilliant concept just made the Internet even less fair than it was before.

Pay-per-click will bring you instant traffic, and it can be very expensive. Still, in some cases, you can see a good return on your investment. In a later chapter, I will show you how you can actually corner certain market shares by using pay-per-click and other methods.

The good thing about the pay-per-click is that some of the engines have a "search term suggestion tool" that allows you to see how many people key in certain words every month. I would recommend using this neat feature to your advantage on all search engines. By using the "suggestion feature" along with the other valuable information you collect, doing a little math and averaging, you can find out how many people actually look for your type of business on the entire Internet.

If one million people key in the key word "cars" on one of the pay-per-click search engines in a month's time—and you know the market share in terms of the numbers of visitors that particular company receives every month—you can find your market share number in terms of a percentage.

After you find your average market share percentage, in terms of specific key words relating to your business, you can take that average to other major search engines and use your individual percentage and compare it to the number of visitors those engines receive every month. You can closely predict how many people actually key in the words you used for your title and description.

You will be surprised how many people do not do the research necessary to have the best search results. As I was writing this section, I did a simple test with one of the search term suggestion tools available online. I keyed in the words "car pricing" and found out that about 4,000 people used those key words during the last month. Not too bad, you might say. Then I did another search for "car price." You wouldn't think there would be that much of a difference, but the words "car price" rather than "car pricing" pulled up about 30,000 results for the same thirty-day period. "How you say something can be just as important as what you say."

At the same pay-per-click search engine, advertisers were paying 54 cents for the key words "car pricing," and advertisers were paying 44 cents per click for the key words "car price." It should be the other way around, don't you agree? You see, people don't know that the market is in the words "car price" not "car pricing" which everyone would expect. While "car pricing" only attracts about 48,000 visitors a year, the key words "car price" receives a whopping 360,000 key word queries every year in this one search engine alone!

The above example shows how only a letter or two can be the difference between a web site that makes a million dollars in sales in a year and one that generates only ten thousand. Do your homework before you spend a single penny. If you cannot figure out how to do it yourself, hire someone who can.

The best thing to do is to use an advertising combination with the search engines. Like the stock market, do not invest all your money in one place, or your successes will be not forthcoming.

Universal Marketing

Once you have your new Internet web site designed and listed in the search engines, it is time to take your business to a new level. But remember, "first things first." Never rely on search engines alone to make your business a success. The search engines should be used as a salesperson to bring in new leads. YOU will be the difference between failure and success, not the search engines.

You have no control over the search engines at all. It is not up to you whether the search engines will even be in business next year. But it is up to you if you want to be in business next year! Your position in the search engine results can be changed, modified, deleted, or removed at any time by these companies.

Credibility

Now it is time to give your company credibility. You can start by offering a 100% guarantee on your products and/or services. All of the companies that I have consulted for have policies that guarantee their products 100%. If you cannot guarantee your products or services 100%, you should not be in business.

Next, you have to make your company interactive with the users. Create an on-line discussion forum and set strict Christian guidelines. If anyone breaks the rules, ban them from your discussion forum.

A successfully operated discussion forum can actually get users to sell your products for you. They do the selling by talking about your products all the time.

A good example of a successful Christian discussion forum can be found at http://www.lloydmiddleton.com/. It is very simple yet effective. There are rules that everyone agrees follow, so it is a very pleasant forum to use. If the company owner also participates in the forum once or twice a week, your users will love it. Try to find ways to bring your web site to life. Let it be a living, breathing entity that wants to grow and interconnect with users.

Placement, Registration, and Marketing Summary Checklist

Search Engines. The checklist below describes the various topics we have discussed in this chapter on search engines. A search engine is a web site destination where millions of people go every day to search for information by keying in a few words and pressing a "Search" button.

Pay Service Registration. If you see any company that says it can register your web site correctly in 1,000 search engines and directories for $99, that company is pulling a fast one on you. Don't give in to this type of misinformation. It will only hurt your listings. Pay the extra fees the large search engines require to do business, and then be sure to study how your competition is listed.

Looksmart™ Registration. Study their submission policies, and study your competition before you register. See what titles and descriptions the top 5 web sites that come up are using. Take your time, and be smarter than the editors that will be judging your web site. You should spend a few days working on your exact title and description. If you do it right, you can secure a good listing on MSN®, AltaVista®, Juno®, Time Warner™, Prodigy™, CNN™, and Excite™ as well.

DMOZ - The Open Directory. It is free to submit to DMOZ. Take your time, review your competition, and try to become an editor in your category to have the inside scoop. DMOZ powers the search results for popular search engines and portals such as Netscape® Search, AOL™ Search, Google™, Lycos®, HotBot®, DirectHit™, and many others.

Yahoo®. Start by doing a preliminary key word search on your business, and see exactly what comes up. In most cases, you will see a category with a few web sites listed under that category. Study your competition, and see what titles and descriptions they have used to make the one to five positions. Sometimes a keyword is in a different category than you might want to register your business in initially. Take your time and study everything that has to do with your competition. Finally, if your web site appears at the middle or bottom of a long list, it might be a good idea to use their sponsorship listings. These listings will immediately place you at the top of the category.

Pay-Per-Click. Use this system to determine market share, because they will surely use you! Pay-per-click will bring you instant traffic, but it can be very expen-

sive. Use every resource you can to your advantage.
Some pay-per- click services have search term suggestion tools. Everything is available for you to figure out
any market share. Be smart, and pay attention, and you
will see that these services are divulging much more
information than most ever realize.

Get Credibility and Have a Personal Touch.
Get credible by offering a 100% guarantee on your
products and/or services. Create an on-line forum, and
have the owners participate. Get personal with your
clients, and offer them something they cannot get anywhere else.

Chapter 7

Final Review

Summary

It seems like it was just yesterday when I made that telephone call to ask Lloyd if he wanted to initiate a unique and different way of doing business. We never forgot where we came from and that every great business started with a great business idea with someone you can trust.

Our whole concept was unique, marketable, and was able to be profitable because of our commitment and dedication to doing whatever it took to get the job done. If you do find that special market that makes you excited every morning when you wake up, you are half way there. If you commit yourself and set realistic goals that can be reached and do whatever it takes to make sure the job gets done, you will be one of the ones who will make it. I never heard of anyone who has failed in business because they were trying too hard.

I believe that everyone has, within, the potential to be self-sustaining, but some people are just not meant to be entrepreneurs. Lets take my brother, for example. He is the hardest workingman I know. He is a plumber by trade, and I tried to get him to start his own business when I first started mine. We are both about the same age; we both love what we do for a living; and we both wanted to be entrepreneurs. The only difference in the paths we chose was that I was willing to risk everything I had, and he was not. Entrepreneurship scared him and excited me. I always believed in myself, and I knew that I would not stop until I reached every goal I set for myself. My brother, on the other hand, always believed in taking the conservative road.

If you choose to try entrepreneurship at some point in your life, you will also cross a path where you have to take a large risk or sacrifice. By carefully analyzing all the factors involved in the actual risk, you can keep it to a minimum.

If you take your time and follow the checklists in each chapter, by using your creativity and unique ideas to either start your new business or expand your existing business, you will have an incredible advantage over your competition and will definitely be headed in the right direction. If I had access to this sort of information before I started in business, I can't even imagine the things I would be doing now.

When you decide to take that first step, make sure you have a qualified person build your web site. This person should be experienced in e-commerce, shopping carts, and basic web site function ability. I would not recommend simply going to the office supply store and buying a program on how to build a web site in 24 hours. You can hire a good quality web site professional to build you a basic start up site for less than one thousand dollars. After it is up and running, you will make many changes until you have it right.

Compare that to the price of purchasing property and having a place of business built on it. You can see how a few thousand-dollar investment is not that bad at all! Once you have the basic web site completed, you can then contract a professional consultant to guide you in the right direction.

If you have the extra time, you can follow the basic guidelines stated in this book and can have a moderately successful e-commerce business. If you do not know where to look, you can log onto our web site at http://www.0to1million.com. We have a section where you can find someone qualified to help get you going.

Get Legal from Day One

I have started several businesses from nothing at all. I remember a certain client, a rather quiet neighbor, who did not even have a computer, but he and his wife wanted to be business owners.

One night, he happened to arrive home the exact time I did, and he said "hi" and asked me what I did for a living. That's pretty much all it takes for someone to ask me. I enjoy what I do so much that I can talk to a complete stranger and convince them that entrepreneurship is an available option for anyone who thinks he or she might have what it takes.

After that initial conversation, this man had a goal in

his mind to be a business owner. He would not stop talking to me about it until I agreed to help him out.

I needed another successful case study for my seminars, so I decided to see how far I could take him with just a few meetings a week. Since he had not even one clue of how a business was supposed to be run, I gave him and his wife a one-hour speech about "Cash Flow" and how it works.

After I drilled them on all the pros and cons of being self employed, it was time for them to pick up the telephone book and contact the business license department located in your state section. I described to them how this first step is needed to open a business checking account and merchant account in order to be able to accept on-line credit card orders.

The only thing they had left to do before all the fun stuff started was to find an office where the business could operate. Since they had no plan on purchasing an expensive office, they decided to start working from home and see what might happen from there. Most homes and apartments are zoned so that you can operate a business in a special area.

You can see how easy starting a business actually can be. My neighbors started their business within two weeks, and they received their first order within one month of listening to my speech on cash flow.

After you make all the necessary calls and have everything in place, you will be legally in business to do e-commerce! Now, you will have to spend a week or two developing a business and/or marketing plan. Don't be afraid to spend the extra time going through this long process. You will thank yourself in the long run for spending the time to establish some direction on where you are going and how you will get there. Try not to expect too much success too fast. If you follow some fundamental guidelines, you are almost there.

Daily Meetings Mean Success

Once you get your business idea off the ground and you already have in your mind that you will go straight to the top, schedule daily meetings with the people that are involved in your business. This interactivity is very useful in getting fast results. By talking to your partners in business on a daily basis on what is to be done next, you will actually discover your business will be much more profitable.

I remember when I initiated an agreement with my largest client. We talked almost every day, and we were more than seven hundred miles away from each other. When the telephone bills became too expensive, we starting using the resources of the Internet. That's what it is there for, so why not use it?

Just about anyone can get a DSL or cable modem connection. When you have two computers with high speed Internet access and you have a copy of the free download Net Meeting installed, you are almost ready for some really neat communications. All you need, then, is to have a few basic things like a headset and a video camera mounted on your monitor. The quality is almost flawless! I cannot believe it is actually free. I use this simple, free system to communicate not only with my most valuable clients but also with family members who are hundreds of miles away. You can see them and talk to them for free, and it is really fun! So, buy a video camera, download a free copy of the software, and you will be ready for the communications your business needs to succeed.

24 Hour Loyalty

One of the important things about e-commerce that is often overlooked is that most people want to do business throughout the world but only want to work from nine to five in their time zone. When I commit and take on a new project, there are no scheduled hours reserved specifically for work. This is the Internet, and the Internet is open twenty-four hours a day three hundred and sixty five days a year!

The good part of the relationship I have with Lloyd, my client and friend, is that I am encouraged to call him any time, day or night. If I see something that needs his attention, I will call him, no matter what time it is—day or night. The orders come in day and night, so we should be available as well.

It is wonderful to be able to log into our web site discussion forum anytime of the day or night, where we always see visitors just chatting away about our products. When you arrive at that point, you can be assured that you are doing everything just as you should be.

Cornering the Market

Imagine being in a unique specialty service market that

relies on sending out thousands of promotional letters a month via first class mail. I know this one man, in particular, who spends up to fifty thousand dollars a year on postage to send out his first class targeted mailings. His market is so specific and unique that he only needs one or two clients a year to make several hundred thousand dollars.

Up until he met me, he would hire a crew of about five or six people every three months to print, stuff, seal, and mail his thousands of sales letters.

When I asked him why he spent so much money on postage, he said, "It is because the people I am looking for have very particular specifications and credentials." "They are companies that gross more than two hundred million a year in sales, and this is just the way I have always done it."

Upon doing some preliminary research, I learned that there were certain key words that only the people who were looking for his services would ever key into a search engine. No one else would ever key in those specific works for any reason.

When I went to some of the pay-per-click engines and keyed in his keywords to see the competition and how much they were paying per click, I noticed it was much less than a first class stamp! By sending out a direct first class mailing to a targeted market, you are actually soliciting them to query you about your services. When a CEO or president of a company keys in a specific key word in a search engine and you come up in the number one position, and it only costs you ten cents opposed to the cost of a first class postage stamp, they are actually looking for you!

If you really examine what I just said very closely, you

would think it should be the other way around. It should cost ten cents to solicit someone and three times that amount to get a "Direct Interest Hit." This is another one of those things on the Internet that not many people catch.

This is the perfect formula someone could use to use to corner a market. If you find that the cost of a direct target hit on one of the pay per click services is much less than the cost for a first class stamp, you have a winning combination for cornering your market while only paying for the people who are really interested in what you have to offer.

In this particular case, we accomplished two different things that deserve recognition. First, the fifty thousand dollar first class postage bill was cut in half by only spending about two thousand dollars a month on a targeted pay-per-click service. Next, the amount of interested people in the service was increased by more than a whopping five hundred percent! Now that's good business!

Enjoy What You Do

Remember that when you select a product or service, you must love and enjoy the business you are about to start. You do not want to be stuck doing something that you dislike no matter how much money it may make you.

Always remember to do your homework on your business and competition, and try to avoid small ticket items unless you have a product that you sell in minimum quantities. The farther away from "Keystone" you are on your profit margin, the less chance you have for success. By sticking to this theory, you can actually eliminate about 70% of all Internet ideas as unfeasible. The better your chances at success, remember to keep a large profit margin and stay close to Keystone.

List-Serve Summary

Don't forget that, when it comes to selling on-line to your customers, you need to offer them something that is very unique and different. If you can offer them something that no one else can offer them, you have just increased your chances of success. Remember that almost anyone can obtain a dealership to sell just about anything. If you find something that is very hard to aquire, you are much better off.

As soon as you have everything all set up and moving forward, you must have a good mailing list program working on your web site. I cannot stress how important it is to have this as part of your successful on-line business.

Once you start using the Internet to explore for about a year or so, you will start receiving e-mail from all types of mailing lists around the Internet.

While there are thousands of newsgroup discussions going on all the time, there are also thousands of e-mail lists that are sent out every day.

The difference between a newsgroup and a mailing list is that you must go to a newsgroup to find the information you are looking for and a mailing list brings the information to you!

Types of Mailing Lists

Mailing lists can be private or public and each particular one usually has hundreds to thousands of subscribers. Let's say that you are interested in baseball cards. You may visit many different baseball card web sites, and you run across one that really catches your attention because they have a monthly mailing list that brings up-to-date information on the baseball trading card industry; you subscribe to it.

If you were the owner of one of the ten web sites that sold baseball cards and had the choice to be one that had no mailing list or you were the one that had a mailing list with ten thousand people on it that were already interested in baseball cards, which business would you want to be?

You would want to be the business that had the mailing list because every time you contacted the ten thousand users on it, you would promote your own products, and it is more than likely that you would sell thousands of dollars in merchandise every time you pushed the button!

I have run many successful mailing lists over the years, and after you do it ten or twenty times, things start to come naturally. You can actually predict how much money will come in just by wording your mailing list letter the correct way. We have a detailed section on how to create the perfect mailing list letter that brings in the most cash on our Web Site. Please feel free to log in and register your copy of this book so you can use our free on-line resources.

For now, the best thing is to take it slow and experiment with your own lists. You will soon become an expert, and you will have a database of what letters work better than others.

When you set up a new mailing list, always have it set to have the list administrator approve every post to the list. This way, you control what is sent out to the users of the list. A perfect case scenario would be to only have your own posts sent out and not allow other registered users to post to the list.

Subscribing to the Mailing List

To join a mailing list, all you need is an e-mail address. To subscribe, you send a message to the list administrator (this is usually not a person, just an automated process), and your e-mail address is added to the list.

I have found, over the years, that the best way to add people to your mailing list very quickly is to give something away for free. Everyone likes something for free! By placing a simple message on the submit form like "By signing up for our mailing list, you will be automatically entered in our monthly contest for one thousand dollars in cash!" this will do two things.

First, everyone at your web site, to begin with, is already interested in your product or service or he/she wouldn't be there. Next, it is your job to capture their e-mail addresses and add them legally to your mailing list because even though they might not have bought something from you this time, if they stay a member of your mailing list, the trend shows that they will actually purchase something from you sooner or later. By using the above technique, you can be assured that you will always have future customers.

To be removed from the mailing list, you have to unsubscribe by sending an e-mail message to the list administrator. Typically, in the body of the message, you type something like "unsubscribe" followed by the name of the list and your e-mail address. The process for removal varies from list to list, but it is usually quite simple. Make sure you remove a user when a request to be removed is made, and your list will be one of the cleanest on the Internet!

The Journey Never Ends

The journey never ends because there is always something more you can do for yourself and for your business to make it more successful. Use my marketing techniques on researching your competition before you even start. You will be much better off by starting a business with little or no competition than you will be if you enter a saturated market that is expensive to operate. In addition, you should try to outsmart your competition by finding ways to sell the same thing a different way and double your traffic and business as I have described throughout this book.

When it is time to name your on-line business, remember that you don't necessarily have to use the same name as your legal "off-line" business name. Try to start the name of your Internet business with the letters "A, B, or C" or a number, as they almost always come up first in the search engines. Internet businesses that start with the letters "X, Y, or Z" almost always come up last in key word searches unless they pay for some additional pay service advertising.

When you are ready to start your business or marketing plan, make a trip to your local office supply store and purchase a business or marketing plan program. It is always a good idea to write down some basic information on a notepad so, when you purchase the program, you can easily transfer the information.

Reviewing the Business / Marketing Plan

Remember to have a cover sheet that includes your business name, address, phone numbers, e-mail and web site addresses

Next, write a detailed business description of your business and how it is expected to work. Include everything you can that draws a clear picture of your business. The more detailed you are, the better off you will be.

Your market analysis page includes the marketability of your product or services. If there is a market for it, do people need it, who would buy it, why would they buy it? By studying the information I have described in the previous chapters, you can actually have a complete marketability and competition analysis of your product. Do as much research as possible, and try to find out as much information you can about your competition. Before you know it, you will be an expert on e-commerce.

Include a section about personnel—you and your responsibilities as well as anyone else involved who would take an active role in your business. When you create the financial section, gather all of your financial records such as credit card, savings, and business checking accounts. It would also be a good idea to have on hand a recent copy of your credit report for your records. Financial institutions will get this information on their own if you are seeking financing, and you do not want to find any unexpected surprises of which you are not aware.

The next section would be about your operating expenses, profit and losses. Provide a detailed list of all your expected operating expenses. Also create a section for your documents that support what you are trying to accomplish. They can include patents, press releases, partners and their financial obligations, etc...

Finally, if you have some good business references that have been in business for a long time and they can say some nice things about you, it would be a good idea to list their names, addresses, and telephone numbers. You should expect every one of them to be called so be careful whom you list. This is not a job application where if things don't work out someone can get fired. This is the big time where a large financial commitment is usually part of any deal.

After you have completed your plan, hire a professional editor or typist to type the entire plan on bond paper. After it has been edited and corrected, it is ready to be printed and published for use. If possible, print your plan with a laser printer on quality bond paper and print about ten copies so you have extras if you ever need them.

Now you can sit back, relax and feel much better about the way you want your business to go because you have an actual plan detailing your strategies.

Cash Flow Review

When it comes to cash flow, the best thing to remember is to pay your bills on time. This will keep you from falling behind on cash flow. Try to plan for them to be received by the vendor one to three days before they are due. When purchasing inventory, try to keep it low by only buying what you need. If your business only has four employees there is no need for ten computers. By only purchasing the supplies you need, you can save needed cash flow every month.

By staying ahead of your receivables (money owed to you), you are insuring cash for your business. Make monthly telephone calls to the people who are late on the money they owe you. When you are late on your telephone bill, the telephone company is the first to let you know. You should let your customers know as well.

If you pay cash for as many things as you can, it will keep you out of serious debt. In addition, if you pay higher monthly payments on your credit cards to get them paid down as quickly as possible, you are increasing your buying power, your credit, and you do not have as much debt.

If you are a large company, you should consider using a secure Intranet system for viewing and printing operational manuals, booklets, etc… Analyze everything you send from one place to another such as schematics, plans, and CAD drawings. Courier services can get very expensive, and if you use a secure Intranet, you can have your information delivered instantly with hardly any cost at all. By using e-mail and video conferencing, your business can save a lot on postage and monthly telephone bills.

Placement, Registration, and Marketing Summary Checklist

A search engine is a web site destination where millions of people go to find information by keying in a few words and pressing a "Search" button. These search engines play an important role in almost all Internet activity.

When it comes time to register your web site in these search engines, start with the ones that have been in business for a long time and have some credibility. Most of them will have a pay-per-click service registration. If you see any company that says it can register your web site correctly in one thousand search engines and directories for $99, don't do it. Don't give in to these services; they will only hurt your listings. Pay the extra fees the large search engines require for business and study how your competition is listed. "It's worth the highest initial investment for quality service."

Finally, try to operate a clean, friendly, honest web site, have faith and believe in yourself.

A lot of people think of the Internet as the place where the entire dot COM's went down, but I see something completely different. The reason some of the multi-million dollar web sites went out of business is not because they were bad business ideas; it was because they had no experience in what they were doing.

For every large dot COM that you have heard of that has gone out of business, I can give you several that were very successful. All of my clients that followed my lead made it big on the Internet, and you can as well.

Conclusion

Every business idea must start somewhere, and the fact that you read this book shows that you are willing to take the first step. You may not be an instant success, but I guarantee that if you pay attention to what you have read and spend the time doing the necessary research before you jump into anything, you will do one hundred times better than someone not knowing what to expect.

We have dedicated a special section on our main web site http://www.0to1million.com that can guide you in the right direction for your endeavors. If you have been in business for many years and you need corporate consulting, or you just want to work at home and bring in an extra income every year, we have something for you.

One of the biggest success stories I have is how my faith in God and myself has spiritually guided me in the right direction. Everyone has their own spiritual beliefs, and one of the most important people you should believe in is yourself. It all starts with a dream and the willingness to go after that dream no matter how long it takes or how many obstacles you have to go through to achieve it!

I am so grateful to have had the opportunity to help so many people and companies over the years that words cannot express my thankfulness. I also feel blessed to be able to help many more people through this book and the Internet resources we have available.

There will be many of you who will catch an untouched, profitable market that not even I have foreseen. Some of you will be searching the Internet for new business ideas and will find out that the business you thought about getting into is actually saturated and expensive. Others will find that the ideas they had are unsaturated and relatively inexpensive. Who knows? Maybe it will be you. Maybe you will be the next person that goes from "$0 to $1,000,000 in 356 days!"

About the Author

I was born February 1, 1968 in Buffalo, New York. I spent the first eight years of my life there, and what I remember most are the very cold winters. When my parents went their separate ways, I moved to West Virginia with my mother and two brothers, Pete and Stuart.

Because my family was rather poor, I had to work twice as hard as other kids just to fit in. While they had money every day for lunch, I had to use those "Free Lunch" tickets that every other poor kid had to use. I used them only a few times, and I remember going hungry because I was so ashamed to use them.

As long as I can remember, I always had a strong desire to be self-employed. Even as a nine-year-old entrepreneur, I would buy a pack of gum for twenty-five cents and sell each of the five pieces for twenty-five cents, making a dollar profit on the pack. Somehow, I always found a way to make money from just about anything.

I was never greedy though; I have always considered myself a generous man and helped my two brothers by paying them to do my chores around the house. I also enjoy helping people out for no reason at all, like my favorite "Girl Scout Cookie Trick," which I began many years ago.

When I visit a store where the Girl Scouts are selling cookies out front, I ask them, "What kind do you think tastes the best?" The girls point out their favorites, and I buy three or four boxes of them. I start to walk away, then suddenly turn back and say, "I forgot—I can't eat chocolate." As soon as they look disappointed, I say, "But you can have them!" Their expressions of delight are wonderful!

Since I was sixteen and able to work, I worked two jobs. Believe it or not, I purchased my first home at age nineteen! All that hard work really paid off.

In the early 1990s, I was in my early twenties and worked for a large photo processing manufacturing facility with about five hundred employees. Everything came so easily to me as I learned new jobs. The company had been in business for about thirty years, and I was somehow able to break every production record that had been set for any machine.

During my seven years of employment with this company, I came up with many ideas for starting my own business, but everyone told me, "This is the best place in town to work; you won't be able to make this kind of money anywhere else."

I was convinced there was a better way, and when I reached the point where I had gone as far as I could go with this company, I decided that was enough! I had enough money to last about a year and decided I could do better, so late one snowy night, I decided to take my chances on my own.

It was one of the most important decisions I have made, and I can't imagine ever pursuing a career other than one of entrepreneurship. Over the years I have personally published more than 50,000 web pages and directories on the Internet and am the holder of two U.S. Patents.

I have had my struggles in business, but I always came through. One of my dearest friends and business colleagues is Lloyd Middleton who shares many of my goals and beliefs. You will have the opportunity to meet him in this book and learn how he has been such an important part of my business success.

The only one I have to thank for my success in business and for the opportunity to help so many people in my personal life is God. He has blessed me since the day I was born, and I have always known it. Someday I will give back all that has been given me! God Bless Everyone.

Best Regards

from the

Author

[signature]

2003